IN
SEARCH

# Shiva

**Haroon Khalid** has an academic background in Anthropology from the Lahore University of Management and Sciences (LUMS). He has been a travel writer and freelance journalist since 2008, travelling extensively around Pakistan, documenting its historical and cultural heritage. He has written for several newspapers and magazines, including *The News, Express Tribune, The Friday Times, Scroll* and *Himal* and is also the author of *A White Trail: A Journey Into the Heart of Pakistan's Religious Minorities*. Born and raised in Lahore he now lives in Islamabad with his wife and works as an educationist. This is his second book.

*Praise for the book*

'Reminds us of roots we tend to overlook.'—Devdutt
Pattanaik

'In the face of rising extremism and intolerance Haroon
Khalid, sets off on a journey in the reverse direction...
exploring Pakistan's folk religious culture and uncovering
its links to Hinduism and history. He then writes a book
with an intriguing title, *In Search of Shiva*.'—*Civil Society*

'Khalid's study lends hope that centuries of folk cultural
traditions might yet be saved from oblivion and provide
a counter-narrative to the rigid interpretation of history
propagated by religious fundamentalists.'—*The News*

'Haroon Khalid introduces the reader to eye-opening
religious traditions in his home country that are rooted
in the cultural beliefs of South Asia.'—*Mid-day*

# IN
# SEARCH OF
# Shiva

## A study of **FOLK RELIGIOUS** practices in **PAKISTAN**

# Haroon Khalid

RUPA

Published by
Rupa Publications India Pvt. Ltd 2015
7/16, Ansari Road, Daryaganj
New Delhi 110002

*Sales Centres:*
Allahabad Bengaluru Chennai
Hyderabad Jaipur Kathmandu
Kolkata Mumbai

ISBN: 978-81-291-3743-2

Third impression 2017

10 9 8 7 6 5 4 3

The moral right of the author has been asserted.

This edition is for sale in Indian subcontinent only.

Printed at Shree Maitrey Printech Pvt. Ltd., Noida

There are a few people in everyone's life who are truly inspirational. For me they are my teachers. They saw immense potential in me, when I couldn't. They taught me that there is more to life than becoming a tool in the machinery of capitalism. They have inspired me and allowed me to see the world in a unique way. I would therefore like to dedicate this book to all my teachers over the years who have taught me to read, write, learn and most importantly, unlearn. This list cannot include all my role models but I have still tried to name a few. They are:

Furrukh Khan
Marta Bolognani
Sadaf Ahmad
Noman-ul-Haq
Rasul Baksh Rais
Pervaiz Vandal
Hassan Karrar
Robeena Tahir
Faiqa Afzal
Samina Rahman
Ahmed Ali
Sir Shaheen
Humair Hashmi

# Contents

# Contents

# Introduction

THIS BOOK IS a product of several journeys, spread over a few years. Some of them were undertaken to write articles, some for research projects, a few as social visits while others for recreation. It is for this reason that my travels in the book are not narrated in a chronological order. I have combined them, scattered over the years, to suit a particular theme. When I compiled these stories I never knew that one day they will all come together in a book. Initially, I did not find any geographical or traditional connection between the different religious practices, but for one, they all represented an alternative version of practised Islam. However, as I came across more such stories I began to notice a common thread that united all of these practices. This was their connection to antiquity. Even though Islamic in its garb, their origins predate the birth of Islam—some of these links go back to the ancient Indus Valley Civilization. In most of these cases, the religious tradition found its roots in the different spiritual traditions that developed around the cult of Lord Shiva. Having been raised in Pakistan, a country that was created out of its opposition to India and Hinduism, this was a fascinating discovery. The religious practices at the shrines were no longer isolated religious practices, but part of a tradition, representing a continuity that the rupture of Partition could not split. They defied the dogma of the exclusivity of the two religions, Islam and Hinduism. They denote that there was much borrowing and lending between different religious traditions and if one is willing to dig beneath the surface these connections can still be found.

I have tried to understand these different religious traditions in the backdrop of the rising tide of religious puritanism and extremism in Pakistan; the creation of Pakistan, the two-nation theory and its economic development. All these factors affect how these shrines are perceived and survive.

Unfortunately due to my limited resources I could not travel as much as I wanted, so there are several areas and shrines that are unexplored and could not be included in this book. Since this was mostly a self-funded project I could only limit my research around my hometown of Lahore. Therefore only parts of central Punjab are included and southern Punjab and Sindh are excluded, where there are many such shrines. These shrines also represent similar characteristics as discussed in this book

# I

# Muslim Rage: Innocence of Muslims

IN PAKISTAN, YOU have the most peculiar national holidays: the death anniversary of a former prime minister, the death anniversary of the mother-in-law of the incumbent president, the birth anniversary of the national poet who died eight years before the creation of this nation, Dengue Awareness Day, etc. And now you have a national holiday 'to protest against the blasphemous movie made by the West'. The movie in question was *Innocence of Muslims* written and produced by Nakoula Basseley Nakoula and directed by Alan Roberts.

Like any other day, I woke up early in the morning on this national holiday of protest, and went for a jog. There was nothing different about the day. The jogging track, as usual, was dominated by post-sixties' health freaks reluctantly dragging their feet, stopping frequently to emphasize a point they had been discussing with their partners. Like many other pleasant national traits, discreetness is not appreciated. The louder one speaks, the greater the claim one has over the truth.

Every morning, I have noticed, the discussion revolves

around religion and politics. Equipped with political views from the late night talk shows that are aired on the dozens of national news channels, the men usually talk about the corruption of politicians. The women prefer to discuss spiritual matters. One frequently hears stories of different prophets mentioned in the Quran, and those of the companions of the Prophet of Islam. Some of the men and women walking alone, carry with them rosary beads, reciting verses from the Quran, while others grip their mobile phones, loudly playing an Arabic recitation of the Holy Book, along with its Urdu translation, a public display of their religiosity. This is a quintessential middle-class park, located in a middle-class locality, in the heart of Lahore. All the walkers come from the surrounding houses, newly built by their children who are working as managers or administrators in big factories and offices.

Today, the discussion revolved around the evil designs of the West to humiliate the Muslim world. As I squeezed past a couple of elderly women, I heard one of them say, 'I don't understand why the Christians have to do this. Have we ever humiliated their Prophet?' The other one responded with an affirmative sound. I wondered if they realized that the 'Christian Prophet', Jesus Christ, is also regarded as a prophet in the Islamic tradition. Disgracing him would also mean committing 'blasphemy' against Islam. Everybody on the track and the ground was inflamed by this movie that they had never seen. Condemning it was their way of taking part in this government-sanctioned protest. Most of them were too old to take to the streets anyway.

The day seemed to drag reluctantly towards noon. There would be some fireworks and fiery sermons from mosque pulpits today. It was a Friday and hence a holy day. Millions of Muslims would gather in their local mosques to offer the obligatory Friday ritual prayer. The prayer would be preceded by a sermon from the local maulvi, who while stroking his oiled beard would pray for the demise of the United States, Israel and India, our own local version of the axis of evil, responsible for everything that is wrong within our country, including suicide bombings, sectarian conflict and a separatist movement in Baluchistan. I remember having a discussion with a friend of mine a few years ago, who after completing his MBA joined one of the largest business organizations in the country. After cracking a series of sleazy jokes, my friend decided to shift the topic of discussion to matters political. 'You know they killed a terrorist in Kurram Agency recently and discovered that he wasn't circumcised. You know what that means? It means that he was a Hindu, an Indian. The Taliban would never kill other Muslims. These are all Indian and Israeli agents pretending to be Taliban, trying to discredit them.' As I rolled my eyes in disgust, having learned by bitter experience that it would not be worth the effort to challenge his contention, my other friends nodded in agreement. I wondered to myself what the authorities were doing inspecting the bomber's penis anyway. My friend took a gulp of beer followed by a drag of charas, and then told us another joke about a Sikh, a Pathan and a Punjabi, and how the Sikh acted goofily and the Punjabi wisely, ignoring the fact that Sikhs and Punjabis can be mutually inclusive.

Later in the morning, I sent a message to my fiancée, Anam, who was using the long weekend to catch up on her reading and writing, to tell her that I would come over after lunch to celebrate the national protest day with her in a somewhat romantic manner. She warned me against it and rightly so. We had no idea what was going to happen. Horrible news was coming in from Rawalpindi and Islamabad. A mob comprising thousands was heading towards the diplomatic enclave to protest outside the United States' embassy. The US government had already stated that it had nothing to do with the private low-budget movie, *Innocence of Muslims*. In fact the US President and the Secretary of State had condemned the movie on several occasions. The recent news was that they were planning to spend thousands of dollars on advertisements to tell the people that the US government condemned the movie. The government of Pakistan, an ally of the US government, had put up barriers to stop the progress of the mob, but for a crowd of thousands these were minor impediments. There were hundreds of foreigners in the diplomatic enclave whose lives would have been under threat if the mob had managed to get past the security.

About a week before, on 12 September 2012, a similar mob had managed to make its way into the US embassy in Libya, resulting in the death of the American ambassador there. The British and German embassies in Sudan were also attacked. In Lebanon, a Kentucky Fried Chicken (KFC) outlet was burned. There were protests and clashes with the authorities in countries such as India, Turkey, Sudan, Tunisia, Nigeria, Sri Lanka, Malaysia, Bangladesh and Indonesia, resulting in the death of hundreds of protestors. This protest brought to mind the agitations against the caricature of the Prophet of Islam published in a Danish magazine a few years before. What these angry protesters failed to realize earlier, and even now, is that their violent protests actually end up reinforcing the very fact that they are protesting. As a result of their aggression, *Innocence of Muslims* became one of the most watched movies on YouTube, with millions of views.

In Pakistan, the protests were being spearheaded by the Islamic parties, both mainstream and those on the periphery, and were being supported by prominent members of society, such as lawyers, journalists, judges, businessmen. A few days earlier, a group of lawyers along with members of religious parties had attacked the US consulate in Lahore, taking down its flag and burning it.

I first heard about the holiday on Thursday, 20 September, a day in advance, when I went to the school where I teach, to conduct my daily class of world history. Interested to know what the schoolchildren thought about this mania that had gripped the Muslim world, I asked them whether they supported the government's decision to announce the holiday and whether they would protest. Salman, one of my most vocal students, immediately raised his hand and said that he would protest by not using Facebook for a day.

'But why would you boycott Facebook?' I asked.

'Because that will hurt their business,' he replied.

'Why do you want to hurt Facebook's business? You do realize it is a separate entity.'

'I want to protest somehow.'

'Who do you want to protest against?'

'The Americans.'

'Why the Americans?' I asked.

'Because they ridiculed our Holy Prophet [Peace Be Upon Him].'

'Are all Americans responsible for that? What about the millions of Muslims living in America?'

'I would only protest against non-Muslims,' Salman said.

'What do Hindus, Sikhs and Buddhists have to do with the movie?' I asked.

'I will only protest against the Christians then.'

'How are all the Christians responsible for what one of them has done? Are we all responsible for what Osama bin Laden has done?'

'No. Then what should I do?' Salman asked.

At about three in the afternoon, taking a risk, I decided to drive to my fiancée's house which is a few kilometres away from mine. Just outside my locality, there was a camp serving milk to the protestors. A banner read that the only punishment for a blasphemer was beheading. Several boys flocked around it for free drinks. I wondered what their motivation was for taking part in this insanity? Recreation? A day out with friends? The boys weren't a day older than fourteen.

A crowd had gathered outside the historic village of Hanjarwal, a village which had been subsumed by the ever-growing metropolis of Lahore. It had seen its share of violence in the past. Temporary gallows had been erected on the road, allowing for traffic to pass on one side. A mob of hundreds had surrounded it, as the smoke of burning tyres spread into the air. An effigy, dressed in a shirt with the US flag on it, was being dragged to the gallows, where some people prepared to hang it. This was going to be a public hanging, a warning to the Western world that this was how Muslims responded to blasphemy. For a moment I felt as if the effigy was alive. An actual person being mortified in public, dying slowly as he was being pushed around, kicked by angry students used to the beatings of their teachers, unemployed college graduates humiliated every day in the search for jobs, businessmen who had suffered in the economic recession.

I could feel his breath being choked out of his throat in anticipation of the death rope around his neck. I could feel my eyes popping out as if I was the culprit being hanged. This wasn't an effigy of the United States or a blasphemer. This was the voice of reason being dragged to death. This was Socrates being given his vessel of poison. This was the Muslim mystic Mansur Al-Hajjaj being cut into several pieces for stating, 'I am the Absolute Truth', a blasphemer. This was Hypatia of ancient Alexandria being dragged by the mob, her clothes tearing away and revealing her naked body to the lustful gaze of the pious believers. This was the start of the end. Such violent responses to provocation would only reinforce the stereotypical image of Muslims as intolerant and would further evoke such provocations. Muslims today face an intellectual challenge which can only be countered through reason, rationality and intellectual discourse. I turned my eyes away from the protesters, afraid that they would be able to read my mind. I was afraid that they would realize that even though I condemned the movie I was not one of these violent protestors.

The next day I came across an interesting article written by a journalist in one of the English newspapers. Even though Friday was declared a national holiday, her office was open. She wrote that on the way to her office, her car was stopped by a group of young boys. One of them raised his stick to smash the car's windscreen. When she jumped out to question him, the boy and the group ran away.

The cover of the following week's *Newsweek* magazine portrayed a photo of Muslim men shouting and protesting. The title read, 'Muslim Rage'.

# 2

# Fertility Cult

I PARKED MY CAR in front of a small dhaba to find out whether the small road led to the village 50 Chak PS.

'Is there a shrine of Aban Shah there?' I asked the owner of the dhaba after he confirmed I was going in the right direction.

'Yes there is,' said the old man sitting on a platform inside.

'See there is a shrine of Aban Shah. I wasn't making it up,' I told my friends as I got back into the car. 'We'll see if they actually have those that you speak of,' replied Maryam, who knew that I was really talking to her, as she had been the most sceptical about the existence of the shrine.

'Penises!' I said with a laugh. Anam, my fiancée and Bilal, a photographer like Maryam, laughed lightly.

In my travels around the country I have seen my share of strange customs and practices that one would not usually associate with Islam, at least with the Islam that I have grown up with. But nothing had prepared me for this, a Muslim shrine dedicated to the fertility cult, where women offer phallic-shaped offerings to the patron saint while praying for a child, ideally a boy. It was a continuation of a tradition that evolved long before the birth of Islam.

Archaeologists have unearthed seals and terracotta figurines from the cities of the ancient Indus Valley Civilization, believed to be part of religious rituals, several of which developed around the fertility cult. There are figurines of pregnant women[1] and seals depicting a male figure sitting in a yogic position with an erect penis.[2] There is consensus amongst archaeologists that these figurines and seals were used as votive offerings to deities while praying for the birth of children. We were on our way to see a tradition that had been passed onto us through a journey of thousands of years.

I was first informed about the shrine by my friend and mentor Iqbal Qaiser. Together he and I had travelled extensively in Punjab, documenting Hindu and Jain temples, gurdwaras and peculiar Muslim shrines located in obscure villages and small towns that do not exist on the political map of the country. His brilliant work, *Historical Sikh Shrines in Pakistan*, documents 135 gurdwaras in the country. Over the years, Iqbal Qaiser has managed to add a new dimension to my understanding of Pakistan and its history, beyond the pitiful state of villages and raw capitalism of towns. He has helped add a historical perspective to my understanding of these places, something that sixteen years of formal education could not do.

A few months prior to my visit to this village, I received a call from Iqbal asking me if he could come and see me. Later in the day, while we were sitting in my garage, around a fire he said, 'Let's make a trip to Pakpattan. There is an interesting shrine there that I want you to see and write about. You know what a *shivling* is, right? There is a shrine there where women worship and present a *shivling* to the grave of the saint. It's incredible, isn't it? A friend came to me in the morning with a "specimen" from the shrine. It was made out of wood and was just like the real deal. I was holding it in my hand when I called you. The shrine is of Aban Shah. My friend told me these penis offerings are lying all over the shrine. They are sacred structures.'

Iqbal Qaiser had also figured out the etymology of the shrine's name by the time he came to me. 'Aban, I think, comes from Abba, the word we use for father.' As it turned out, Iqbal Qaiser couldn't make the trip to the shrine with me because he was busy.

Prominent Indus Valley archaeologist Mark Kenoyer is of the opinion that the seals depicting a nude male figure with an erect penis sitting in a yogic position, discovered from Mohenjo-daro, could actually be a prototype of Lord Shiva, one of the most important Hindu deities. In Hinduism, Shiva is depicted as a lingam which is a phallus. In Hindu temples, the lingam is placed inside a structure called yoni, signifying the vagina. Together they represent the divine power of procreation. In most religions, God is seen as a creator as well as a great father. In the context of this particular shrine, the saint is viewed as someone who bestows birth therefore a father figure.

Mahadev Chakravarti in his book *The Concept of Rudra Śiva Through the Ages*, mentions that in post-Vedic[3] literature, Shiva is known as the god of procreation.[4] He further explains that in an agriculture-intensive society like that of the Indus

Valley (similar to present day Punjab, Pakistan) the fertility cult has particular significance, as cultivation is perceived to be an act of procreating. He writes that Shiva is also worshipped as the god of cultivation. In post-Vedic literature one finds the river Ganges on top of Shiva's head emphasizing his fertilizing power.[5]

Fertility cults have played a prominent role in all ancient civilizations. In Egyptian civilization, there were Khem and Osiris, in Assyrian there was Vul. Fertility rituals developed around Pan and Dionysius in Greece, Fricco in Scandinavia, Hortanes in Spain, Adonis in Phoenicia and Attis in Phrygia.[6] Several of these ancient cults developed in isolation, without much sharing and borrowing from each other, highlighting humans' fascination with the process of creating and creation. The fertility cults also represent the human quest to leave a mark on the world, to become a creator himself/herself through his/her progeny, a lack of which therefore, requires divine intervention. Fertility dominates human existence, whether it is in the form of humans, being an act of creation, or creators depicted in art, music, etc.

'Is this shrine something like the Kanamara Matsuri?' asked Maryam as we headed towards the village. It was a single road, with its edges tethered, as if bitten off by some prehistoric monster and then discarded because of its bad taste. Frequently we would have to climb down on the road to give way to a trolley and a tractor overflowing with sugarcane.

'What is Kanamara Matsuri?' asked Anam.

'It is a festival held each year at a shrine in Japan with the penis as the central theme. The name of the shrine is Kanayama, which too is a penis-venerating shrine,' I replied.

'I really want to go there sometime for the festival,' commented Maryam.

'I want to take back souvenirs to show to my friends,' she added.

Staring out into the deep fields on a bright afternoon, Bilal smoked away.

'Me too,' Anam joined her in excitement.

'They'll let us do that, right?' Maryam wanted to know.

'Of course they will. They will be lying all over the shrine. We can just pick one up and take it back,' I said with assurance.

The concrete road gave way to a mud track as we entered the village. It was smaller than I had expected, a few hundred houses, most of which were made of mud, just like villages and cities would have looked in the Indus Valley Civilization. It was deserted except for a few naked children running along our car, a rare sight in this secluded part of the village. Under the shade of a house, I noticed a group of elderly men gathered around a hookah, adjusting their glasses and peering closely at us 'strange creatures'.

We left behind a trail of dust and continued looking out for any signs of the shrine. The mud track gave way to a concrete road as we left behind the last remaining row of village houses. I stopped a young man approaching us on a cycle and asked him about the shrine. He pointed towards a graveyard, off the concrete road. The shrine was surrounded by a cluster of trees. Socially appropriate I thought, imagining phallus structures hanging from the branches. There was a modest house next to the shrine.

As we parked our car next to this house, a child peeped out, probably curious about the strange sounds. The shrine was an unassuming building, a lonely structure in the graveyard. It was single-storeyed with a green dome on top of a white body. Baba Aban Shah was scribbled at its entrance. A small courtyard stretched out in front of the shrine, with remnants of a boundary wall around it. White turbans with festoons and glass bangles were scattered at the other end of the courtyard. These two objects symbolize the groom and the bride. They must have been placed there by supplicants hoping to get married. There were no signs of any phalli. My friends spread out across the graveyard, while I entered the shrine. The grave, without any identifying plaque, lay at the centre of the room, with a bowl of salt, to be consumed by devotees for blessings, next to it. Still no phalli.

Outside, my friends were disappointed after searching vainly all over the graveyard.

'At least we will get to see Baba Farid's shrine at Pakpattan,' I said, trying to cheer them up. Maryam gave me an I-told-you-so look.

As we turned despondently towards the car, I realized that we had overlooked an old lady who had come out of the house and was standing next to the car, with one hand placed on the child who had first appeared when we parked there. She was about seventy and looked like she had seen poverty all her life.

'Where are you from? Why don't you come inside?' she told us.

We followed her. She took us to a portico where another old woman was lying on one of the several charpoys (rope beds). A young boy of eighteen with a shaved head, sat next to her. He seemed lost in his own world and didn't look at us as we entered. We were told later that he was mentally disturbed.

Two males and two females, we could have easily been newly married couples seeking the blessings of the saint to have a child. I explained to the woman lying on the charpoy that we were there to seek the blessings of the saint. She appeared satisfied with my explanation.

'I moved into this house a few years ago after the death of my husband, who is buried in the graveyard outside. I have two children, one of them is this boy. He is a Saeen.[7] I am crippled and after the death of my husband I had no place to go so I came and settled here, next to his grave.'

Her name was Hajra. Not knowing how to ask these two women about the phalli offerings, I asked them about the bangles and the turbans instead.

'These are presented to the shrine by women praying for children. Some of them also bring toys for children and tie them around the trees outside. Not all of them come to ask for children of their own. Women sometimes come to pray for their cows to give birth to calves.'

Hanifa, the old woman who had brought us in, nodded in agreement.

Offering toys and seeking blessings from sacred trees is another tradition that has continued from the religious practices of the Indus Valley Civilization. Archaeologists and historians have identified a few of the figurines discovered from Indus Valley cities as toys, which could have been offered to deities with a specific purpose.

It seems as if thousands of generations have survived in this very form.[8] Peeling off the layers of this civilization, we find that it is the same people with similar beliefs who live here today. The changes that have occurred have only been on the surface, sometimes taking the form of paganism, sometimes that of Buddhism, to be replaced by Jainism, Hinduism and then Islam. Several trees have also been depicted in the votive seals with deities, leading experts to assume they were also allotted special religious significance. The most important one was the banyan tree, which is still considered sacred in the Hindu, Buddhist and even Muslim traditions of South Asia, something that these religions have adopted from the Indus Valley Civilization. The *waan* trees stooping over the graves outside are also considered sacred in the Muslim saints' hagiography. These trees are known to live through several centuries and are associated with several miracles.

'My brother told me that this is not the actual grave of the saint and that Aban Shah was not his real name,' added Hanifa.

She confirmed Iqbal Qaiser's thesis that Aban Shah was not a name but a title given to the saint for the effectiveness of his blessings on childless couples.

'His real name was Baba Lal Shah. He once came here and tied his horse to the *waan* tree next to the shrine. While he was staying here the horse died so the saint buried it and moved on.'

Historically, Muslim mystics have preferred itinerant lives which allow them to learn about spiritual matters from different sources, and also to proselytize. Jürgen Wasim Frembgen, a leading scholar on Muslim culture, compares the itinerant nature of a mystic's life to the metaphorical journey that humans undertake at the time of their birth till their death, considered to be their final destination.[9]

'He is actually buried in a village called Lakhewali Haveli near Pakpattan next to the river [Sutlej]. I have never seen that shrine myself but my brother has.'

'So women offer turbans, bangles and toys to the shrine. Is there anything else that they offer?' I asked Hajra, wondering if by asking this question I had crossed the line of social decorum. I had tried to be as tactful as possible. Hajra covered her face with her dupatta and giggled whereas Hanifa gave a coy smile while slapping the little boy gently on the back.

'Yes, yes,' replied Hajra. 'Women also sometimes offer *killis* to the shrine. We place them inside now because children would often run off with them.'

*Killi* in Punjabi is used as a slang to refer to a nail, specifically one which is inserted into a particular surface like a wall or a cupboard to hang pictures or clothes. I assumed that the *killis* Hajra was referring to were phallus offerings.

'You might find a few tied to the trees outside as well. Women tie them to the branches praying for a child,' added Hanifa.

'No, you won't find any on the trees. I removed them all and placed them inside. They would get lost otherwise. Children and young boys who do not know their importance play with them and then take them away. We lost so many like this that I now protect all of them. Whenever any new *killi* is presented I collect it and save it,' said Hajra.

The fact that out of all the offerings—toys, bangles and turbans—presented to the shrine, children would choose to pick up the *killis* also meant that they understood what they symbolized. It wasn't out of fear of theft that Hajra was hiding them but out of concerns of modesty. Morality defined by a more urbane Islam had finally caught up with this particular practice as well.

'How long have you been collecting them?' I asked her.

'Ever since I moved here. I now have a bag full of them inside,' she said, pointing to a room behind her which had no door.

'Can I see one?'

'Of course! Hanifa go inside and bring one from a black bag.'

A few minutes later Hanifa emerged with a *killi*, about six–seven inches in length, and gave it to Maryam and Anam to examine. It was a simple wooden structure that could be passed off as a penis with some imagination.

'Can I see any of the other ones?' I asked Hajra.

'They are all the same. Just look at this one.'

I didn't want to test the limits of Hajra's hospitality so I conceded.

'Most of the visitors to the shrine are jungli from the neighbouring village. They bring all these things and present them. We are migrants. We don't believe in such traditions,' said Hajra with an apologetic tone.

Why was she protecting them, I wondered, but refrained from asking her.

Jungli, which literally means 'people of the jungle', is a popular term used to refer to the indigenous Punjabis, as opposed to those who settled here after the construction of the canal colonies by the British during the late nineteenth and early twentieth centuries. Using ingenious methods of civil engineering, the British connected the five rivers of Punjab with each other through canals, turning several acres of jungle land into agricultural land. As a result, thousands of new villages, referred to as *chaks* were established, and farming families from all over Punjab were invited to settle in these villages and tend the land. One such village was 50 Chak PS. The former inhabitants of the areas where the *chaks* were established were primarily nomads who did not have the concept of private ownership and were thus unable to prove ownership over land that they had lived on for thousands of years. Their land was snatched away and allotted to these migrants. Soon their nomadic lifestyle came to be referred to as uncivilized or jungli.

There was a subtle implication behind this otherwise harmless sounding remark. Hajra wasn't using the word jungli as a derogatory title, but rather as a means of identification. However, the distinction was raised to dissociate with the shrine and its 'vulgar' practices, a distinction which was necessary due to our presence. Given her ignorance of our religious leanings, she wanted to distance herself from this paganism, which would normally offend the sensibilities of most religiously inclined city-dwellers. Even though both women didn't say anything, I wondered if there had been any backlash from the conservative elements of the village resulting in them taking a defensive stance.

All the inhabitants of 50 Chak PS were from the wave of the second migration that took place after the division of Punjab between India and Pakistan. As opposed to the migrants who had suffered at the hands of the Hindus and the Sikhs during the riots, the locals all over the country generally tend to be more embracive of practices 'non-Muslims'. I have seen several gurdwaras and temples being taken over and destroyed by the migrants who moved into them after losing their homes and belongings in India. On the contrary, in villages and towns where a considerable percentage of the population is indigenous, such 'non-Muslim' religious spaces are better looked after. This is primarily due to a historical bond developed over several generations. However, there are exceptions, and there have been several occasions in which the indigenous have been as brutal to non-Muslim shrines as any other community. This particular village's inhabitants were predominantly Hindus and Sikhs, abandoned following the riots of 1947. In contrast, the neighbouring village housed Muslims who had lived there for several generations and who must have developed a particular association with this shrine, a religious space that they must have shared with Hindus and Sikhs. For the migrants, such a local fertility cult would have been scandalous and therefore, must have taken some time to find place in their religious sensibilities. But given the fact that Hajra was based here and collected the offerings to maintain their sanctity, meant that the cult was able to grow popular among the newcomers as well.

'We don't know how old this shrine is. It was present here before the creation of Pakistan,' said Hanifa, whose family had moved here after the Partition. Hajra's ancestral roots also lay on the other side of the divide.

'You know the saint is responsible for maintaining the purity of his own shrine. He can read everyone's intention. If you come with evil intention he will emerge as a lion and devour you. I have seen it with my own eyes,' said Hanifa. 'There are also several snakes here that guard the shrine and bite only those who are evil. If you are pure of heart nothing will happen to you even if they crawl up your leg.'

There was a sense of urgency in her tone, a justification of sorts that phallus offerings don't represent a corrupt moral system. Rather it is a holy act, and if anyone tries to trivialize it, the person is punished severely. I thought about my conversation with Maryam in the car and hoped for the sake of our safety that the story was just superstition. I wondered though, if the saint had promised to protect his own shrine, why was Hajra intervening by protecting the offerings.

By talking about the snakes around this fertility shrine, Hanifa, without being aware of it, had made an age-old connection between fertility cults and snakes. Snakes, because of their ability to shed their old skins and grow a new one, are seen as symbols of rejuvenation and everlasting youth. In Hinduism, Shiva worship and worship of a snake go hand in hand. In seals discovered from Mohenjo-daro, which are believed to represent the proto-Shiva, the figure is flanked by two kneeling snakes. Even in the Mahabharata, an epic read and revered by Hindus, snakes are closely affiliated with Shiva. In fact, one of the several incarnations of Shiva is that of a snake god. There are similar connections between snakes and fertility cults in other ancient religions. Osiris, a god from ancient Egypt, and the Greek god of Hermes, both known for their fertility power, are shown holding snakes.[10]

On the way out, I noticed several burrows dug by snakes. Perhaps in earlier days, devotees coming to seek the blessings of Saint Aban Shah also had offered milk and prayed to the snakes of the saint, a tradition which then fizzled out and died, similar to what would eventually happen to the phallus offerings.

Feeling parched, we stopped for drinks at the only shop in the village on our way back from the shrine. A group of children gathered around us. Standing behind the counter was thirty-year-old Akhtar, equally intrigued by our presence. There was a television set placed on a high plank in this small room, one of the few technological advances that had trickled down to villages. This harmless-looking box has revolutionized the culture of faraway villages. It has brought to them the message of uniform nationalism, the dictates of a pure religion purged of its past corruptions that had 'seeped into it during its days of interaction with the Hindu culture'. It has brought to these villages new ideas of what civilization and civilized mean, resulting in the reinterpretation of their own worldview. I had no doubt that this harmless-looking box had played a pivotal role in inviting disdain towards the shrine of phallic offerings.

Akhtar had a short beard, a symbol of religious piety. 'Please ask this lady to go away,' he said, referring to Anam who was standing next to me while we were talking to him about the shrine.

On a normal day, Anam would have been enraged by such sexist behaviour and would have probably given Akhtar a piece of her mind. Today she left us to interview a local woman.

'The truth is that a few years ago, the elders of our village decided to remove all these things [killis] from the shrine. This is because young girls were being corrupted due to the practices there.'

I understood why he had asked Anam to leave. He was afraid that she might get 'corrupted' as well.

'Girls would collect these offerings and engage in immoral activities. So finally it was decided that only those particular offerings, the *killis*, needed to be stopped whereas anything else could be presented to the shrine. Now no one presents the *killis* there.'

I wondered if Akhtar knew about Hajra's preservation and decided against telling him about it.

Female sexuality has always threatened the male's sentiment in religious stories. One would come across several narrations of male yogis, saints and mystics being incited by celestial nymphs while they meditated. Perhaps the most famous of them was Buddha. In the Islamic tradition, it is the sexuality of the female that is to be guarded as it has the potential to disrupt the senses of a male. The story of Prophet Yousuf comes to mind—in this story, the Egyptian wife of his master was so enthralled by his beauty that she made several attempts to have a sexual relationship with him and when that failed she got him punished by making up stories against him. This concept of female sexuality, untamed and beyond control, is a recurring theme in ancient religions. I was glad Anam was not around to hear this version of the story.

Akhtar's testimony presented the larger picture. Hanifa and Hajra had earlier said that the saint himself was responsible for protecting the holiness of his own shrine, which essentially meant that he didn't require human intervention to restore moral order, which was what the 'elders of the villages' (who must have been all men, of course) were primarily doing. Images of the saint taking up the form of a lion and attacking those who played around with the phalli came to my mind. Even though these two women had conceded to the wishes of the elderly, they had also developed a counter-narrative which said that there is no need for such an intervention. How superficial then was Hajra's claim that only the jungli took part in this practice. Of course, the women of this village believed in this cult.

My analysis was further strengthened by the story of Salma, a twenty-five-year-old housewife whose family had moved to this village from Ferozepur district, India. She had three children, two sons and a daughter, all of whom she believed were born after seeking the blessings of Aban Shah. Salma told Anam separately while I was talking to Akhtar, that when she hadn't conceived after five years of marriage, her mother-in-law had threatened her with divorce. Out of desperation, she presented a phallus offering to the shrine and was rewarded with three children. Now she visits the shrine regularly. In fact while she was pregnant, Saint Aban Shah appeared in her dream and suggested the names of the children. She also repeated the stories about the saint appearing as a lion to protect the sanctity of his shrine. It amazes me how miracles occur despite all odds because of the power of faith.

As we headed out of the village, a group of children ran after our car. I wondered how many of them were products of the blessings of Saint Aban Shah.

≈

'Jihad an obligation, now or never' read an advertisement, sponsored by the Jamaat-ud-Dawa, on the back of a rickshaw. Underneath it was a gruesome picture of a bloodied hand covered by the American flag, cut through by a sword which was in a hand covered by the Pakistani flag.

'They plan to fight the Americans with swords,' I joked with Iqbal Qaiser, who grumbled and refused to comment. He lacks a sense of humour when it comes to religious violence and exploitation.

We left the Multan Road highway, a four-lane motorway running from Lahore to Karachi, and took a more modest road towards Chechawatni. Our guide was Altaf, a friend of Iqbal Qaiser who was from a neighbouring small city. Altaf had told us about another shrine similar to the one at 50 Chak PS, also called Aban Shah. I didn't assume these two shrines were related. Instead I thought that both of them must have developed independently, adopting the name Aban Shah because of its etymology. From Kamalia we picked up Nauman, a cousin of Altaf who knew the exact location of the shrine.

'Don't tell them you are here to write about the shrine,' Nauman warned us. He had returned only a couple of days before from Hajj, and was still under the spiritual aura acquired from that experience. His expressions and the way he talked about the shrine gave away the fact that he didn't have much sympathy for such a practice justified in the name of Islam, but he didn't express it.

'Tell them instead that you are devotees and have come here to seek the blessings of the saint. I'll talk to them and see if they will allow us to take photographs.'

'A few months ago some journalists who were trying to photograph the shrine were attacked by the guardians there. They broke the cameras as well,' said Altaf.

'They also had a fight with the students from a newly

constructed Ahle-Hadith madrassah in Kamalia. From what I have heard, these students went to the shrine and stole that thing from there and came back to the city. The devotees of the shrine are all Ahle-Tashi [Shias] and when their guardian found out that the madrassah boys had run away with the penis [Nauman seemed rather amused at the practice and enjoyed using the word *lun* for penis] they gathered their followers and came to their madrassah here, picked up the boys and beat them up. They got back their object.'

This sounded rather fascinating. I had always assumed that Shias would be subjected to aggression because Pakistan is a Shia-minority country. However, here, the Shias were able to muster enough strength to fight to keep alive a particular tradition.

'Are the Shias in majority here?' I asked them.

'They are equal, 50-50. The Ahle-Hadith is a minority though,' explained Altaf.

The Ahle-Hadith is a puritanical reformist movement developed in the nineteenth century in the Indian city of Bhopal, to purge 'unlawful innovations'[11] in Islam. Historically, the Ahle-Hadith have had limited influence in Pakistan with only 6 per cent of religious seminaries belonging to this particular school of thought.[12] However, in the past couple of decades this particular brand of Islam has been expanding its scope in the country. From 1988 to 2000, the number of Ahle-Hadith seminaries has increased by 131 per cent.[13] The percentage increase since 2001 is likely to be even more than this. This group maintains close links with Saudi Arabia (Wahhabi Movement), which funds their projects in Pakistan. The movement gained momentum during the

Afghan jihad against Soviet occupation in the eighties. Their ideological inclinations are closer to the Wahhabi and the Salafi movements. Many radical Muslim groups are, ideologically speaking, Ahle-Hadith—one of the most prominent in Pakistan is the Lashkar-e-Taiba, notorious for its militancy in Indian–controlled Kashmir. After the group was banned in Pakistan it adopted the title of Jamaat-ud-Dawa.

The Jamaat-ud-Dawa has in the past couple of years gained much popularity across the urban landscape of Pakistan primarily due to its philanthropy and campaign for populist political demands. It was at the forefront of protests when Pakistan gave India the most favoured nation status in 2011. This organization was also at the vanguard of the protests that followed the blasphemous movie *Innocence of Muslims*. One of the most pressing concerns has been the newly acquired reach of the organization into rural Pakistan, which accounts for a major part of the country. All over the countryside, I came across graffiti against India and the US whereas earlier one would have found announcements of saints' festivals.

This is the first Ahle-Hadith seminary in Kamalia and its ideology is still followed by a minority, but with the way Pakistani society is turning towards a puritanical Islam, this school of thought is likely to have a more sympathetic audience in the future.

'I'll tell you about an incident,' said Iqbal Qaiser. He often gave me lessons on history in this particular manner. 'Once, a Muslim went to a Hindu moneylender and borrowed some money. When he couldn't repay the loan, he went to the local muezzin and devised a strategy with him to cheat the moneylender. The muezzin, using the mosque loudspeaker, announced that the Hindu moneylender had adopted Wahhabism. The people of that city, Muslims included, hated Wahhabis so much that they stopped going to the moneylender. People [Muslims] would rather go to a Hindu back then than a Wahhabi.'

I doubted the veracity of the story but it was useful because it explained the attitude of the locals.

Altaf and Nauman decided to show us a Hindu temple before heading out to the shrine. In the outskirts of the city, we stopped in front of a dilapidated building. Knee high grass greeted us. Iqbal Qaiser and I quickly began to analyze the architectural features of the structures to impress our hosts, as if their hospitality depended on our ability to identify the British era from the Sikh.

'The main building has thick bricks which means this was constructed during the British era,' began Iqbal Qaiser.

'The small structure on the side is from the Sikh era. Do you see the thin bricks? These were used before the British. This must have been a samadhi of an important priest,' I quickly added, too egoistical to stay out of the discussion.

An ancient peepal tree stood in the middle of these two structures. The tree must have been part of the religious rituals of the temple, like it is now in Muslim shrines. We rather expertly directed the attention of our 'students' towards the faded frescoes, but I could tell that they weren't interested any more. Nauman left us pretending to make a phone call while Altaf went for a smoke, trying to be deferential by not smoking in the precincts of the temple. I knew that religious sensitivity was the least of his concerns. He was looking for some respite from his didactic companions.

A small government school was located behind the temple, but it was shut. Its finely maintained structure was in sharp contrast to the fading temple in the background. Shattered pieces of bricks from the temple were scattered on the empty ground of the school. Iqbal Qaiser and I concluded that the school was constructed on this abandoned temple, a precious piece of property that would have been too tempting to abandon. Ironically, while the majority of Pakistani students spent their entire lives without seeing a Hindu temple, these students were studying in the backyard of one.

≈

The shrine of Aban Shah was located high in the middle of a *pahari* now being used as a graveyard. It looked like the sort of *pahari* that hid secrets of an ancient settlement waiting to be unearthed. A long time ago, before the science of archaeology was introduced to Indians, the *pahari* was converted into a graveyard, forever enclosing its secrets. The shrine constructed around the grave of the saint was a colourful, well-maintained structure. Another similar structure, white in colour standing behind it, was said to belong to a descendant of the saint.

Watching us approach, a scrawny old man, started playing his dhol while some children danced in front of him. Iqbal Qaiser and I sat in front of the shrine along with other devotees and *malangs* (Muslim mystics), while Nauman and Altaf walked up to a young man supervizing the painting at the shrine.

'They are preparing for the *urs* [annual festival],' yelled an old *malang* sitting next to us.

'They won't allow you to photograph the shrine but you

can take pictures of these graves and can ask questions,' said Nauman as he came back dejected.

'Please don't mind,' said the young man. He was the current guardian of the shrine. 'Actually a few months ago, some television journalists came here. They interviewed me and shot everything. I tried explaining our traditions and customs to them but when they aired the news feature it was very different from what we had expected. As it was likely to invite a backlash we decided after that incident that we will not allow any video or photograph of the penis. I'll be happy to answer your questions though,' he said.

For the young journalists raised in a strict religious environment, reporting this exotic tradition would have been influenced by their own versions of Islam, in which phallic offerings would be an unlawful corruption of religion instead of a cultural deviancy. As I was about to start my series of questions, the young man received a call and told us that he needed to leave. However, he invited us to his *dera* in fifteen minutes.

I tried engaging one of the old *malangs* in a conversation but his accent was too stilted for me, so I had to ask Iqbal Qaiser to act as a translator. After talking briefly about the miracles of the saint, I asked the *malang* if the magical phallus was present at the shrine.

'It's locked inside and the keys are with me.'

He looked like someone who belonged to a generation innocent of deceit, when miracles happened and religious violence was unimaginable.

'Can I see it?'

'Sure!'

'Darbar Aban Shah Shirazi', read the inscription at the entrance to the shrine, Shirazi signifying that he belonged to the city of Shiraz in Iran, the heart of Shiism. The grave of the saint lay in the centre of the room covered with a cloth decorated with verses of the Quran composed with a golden thread. A small lock hung on a blue box fixed to the ground. The old *malang* opened the box and took out a phallus-shaped object, leaving the money lying next to it untouched. It was a wooden structure, about eight inches long, painted half in blue and circumcised from the top, unlike the phallic offering I had seen at the earlier Aban Shah shrine.

'This is rubbed on the stomach of a barren woman and then she bears children like fertile land produces wheat,' said the *malang* while we inspected the phallus.

Next, we headed towards the guardian's residence, about a kilometre away from the shrine. His name was Syed Faheem Abbas and he told us he was twenty-five years old. His residence depicted prosperity in that humble village. The house was constructed around the shrines of his father, grandfather and great-grandfather, all of them guardians of the shrine of Aban Shah during their lifetime. In an open space on the other side, there was a small stable with four horses. A black flag on top of a hand-shaped poll stood next to the shrine. This is a Shia symbol.

'One of our devotees has gifted us a horse,' said Faheem. 'Let me show it to you.'

Faheem had mistaken Iqbal Qaiser and me for Shias. The votive threads and bangles on my wrist and Iqbal Qaiser's speech interspersed with Shia terminology had probably fooled him. Nauman and Altaf were amazed at our ability to befriend him when they had failed. He took us behind the shrine to a room where a beautiful white horse was tethered.

'We have bought a UPS for the horse, so that its fan continues to function when the electricity shuts off.'

The horse has particular significance in the Shia tradition. It symbolically represents the horse of Imam Hussain, the grandson of the Prophet of Islam, who was assassinated in the month of Muharram. The horse is considered holy, and unlike ordinary horses, it is interred after its death.

Faheem's lifestyle showed that being heir to a shrine had monetary benefits. While the puritanical versions of Islam exploit the religiosity of the people in the name of true Islam, urging them to be violent, such syncretistic traditions have their own mechanisms of exploitation.

'The shrine of Syed Aban Shah Shirazi is about 350 years old,' said Faheem as we sat down to talk. 'The saint's father's name is Syed Lal Esan Shah who migrated from Shiraz. He had three wives, one belonged to a Syed family, the second to a Mir family and the third one was a Kharal.'

Each wife was from a different caste. The Syeds are said to be the progeny of the Prophet of Islam. In the esoteric tradition, their direct lineage from the Prophet gives them access to spiritual insights. In the folk religion that has developed around Islam in Pakistan, one's claim to a Syed family ensures societal as well as religious status. In a lot of cases, the religious status is used as an economic ladder. In the caste tradition of folk Islam, they are the highest caste. Faheem had also cashed in on his Syed caste. He used Syed as part of his name because of its importance. Syed Faheem Abbas. Some male members of the Syed family who do not use the title of Syed in their names sometimes prefer another one called Shah. So the name Aban therefore becomes Aban Shah.

On the other hand, the two castes, Mir and Kharal, are both indigenous to South Asia, with the Mirs deriving their ancestry from Kashmir and Kharals from Punjab. In the Hindu traditional caste system, both these castes belong to the upper echelons. The Mirs trace back to Hindu Brahmins and Kharal to Hindu Rajputs.

'Syed Lal Esan Shah had a total of five children, three from his Syed wife and one each from Mir and Kharal. Baba Aban Shah was the son of the Kharal wife. One night, Syed Lal Esan Shah woke up at night to offer his Tahajjud[14] prayers. He asked his sons from the Syed wife to prepare his prayer mat and fetch water to perform ablution. It was the middle of the night and all of them were sleepy so they refused to comply with his command. The other two sons in the meanwhile woke up. While one of them fetched water for his father the other laid out the prayer mat. Enraged by the insolence of his three sons Syed Lal Esan Shah cursed them. He said:

*Fareed Gharib* [Fareed, you will remain poor]
*Ghaus marchade dhos* [Ghaus, you would be subjected to fraud]
*Dadu tenu bhok kabo* [Dadu, you would be controlled by hunger]

Syed Lal Esan Shah then blessed his other two devoted sons. He said that the son from the Mir wife would rule the river Ravi, and now his shrine stands in the middle of the river a few kilometres from here. Whereas the surrounding area gets flooded during the monsoon, the shrine always remains protected. I have seen it with my own eyes. It is a miracle. His progeny also bears two marks on the forehead depicting horns. Syed Lal Esan Shah forgot to bless Baba Aban Shah. After a little while, Baba Aban Shah asked his father, "What do you have for me, *lun*?"[15] "And then that would be your gift," said Syed Lal Esan Shah. "Your progeny would belong to every caste, from fakir to peasant to a landlord, etc. They would spread all over." And that prophecy has come true. Now Baba Aban Shah has devotees all across the length and breadth of Pakistan, people who belong to all castes. Syed Lal Esan Shah's Syed progeny lives in the neighbouring areas in a bad state. The curse of the Baba still holds true.'

As Faheem narrated the apocryphal story of his ancestors, I couldn't help but marvel at the underlining sociological phenomenon imbibed in its folk origin. Conventionally, the Syed sons, because of their higher religious caste, would have succeeded the spiritual tradition of their father, but this folk story challenged their normal undisputed claim to spirituality. Instead, it elevated individuals who belonged to the indigenous castes of South Asia. The story is a subtle critique of the hegemony that the Syed typically have over spiritual matters. However, that was clearly not how Faheem understood the story. Unconsciously criticizing the concept of Syed-hood, he fell back on his own Syed-ness when he needed to derive his spiritual legitimacy.

'Recently a woman from Karachi presented the shrine a penis made of marble. It is beautiful,' said Faheem.

'May I see it?' I asked.

'I am sorry. That would not be possible. You see there are

a few segments in society which are strongly opposed to our tradition. These are primarily people from the Ahle-Hadith, who have recently set up a madrassah in Kamalia. About two years ago, young passionate students of the institution attacked this shrine and broke the box which keeps all the penises, with a rod. They took the offerings to the city. The *malangs* and other devotees who were present at the shrine followed them and got hold of them, bringing them back here. We locked and beat up the students. There was another similar attack about a year ago but once again the *malangs* defended the sanctity of the shrine. These people say this is an immoral shrine. They are busy propagandizing against us in the city, trying to get the people to turn against us. Because of this fight with the Ahle-Hadith, the number of visitors to the shrine has decreased drastically. Earlier we would hang all the offerings on the trees around the shrine but ever since this conflict, we have been instructed by a senior police officer from the city to stop displaying them to maintain peace. It was then that we decided to stop showing them to visitors. Only those coming to ask for a child get to see them.'

This is the typical attitude of the authorities. In a sectarian conflict like this one, they tend to sympathize with the group towards which they are religiously inclined. In a country like Pakistan, religious neutrality has become impossible to maintain. Judges, lawyers, politicians and policemen, all have their religious inclinations which they exhibit when confronted with an issue of sectarian conflict. When the minaret of an Ahmadi place of worship[16] bothers the sensitivity of pious Muslim believers, the authorities ask them to remove the minaret to maintain peace instead of allowing them to practise their religion independently. Similarly, here, the senior police official succumbed to the pressure of the majority Muslim group instead of protecting the religious freedom of a fringe group. In the name of peace, the minority group gives up its religious traditions and symbols, instead of the majority group being asked to give up its pathological hatred.

'You know it is good that you don't hang it openly now. It doesn't look good,' commented Nauman, whose religious sensibilities clearly went against such practices.
Faheem ignored his observation.

'So how does the phallic tradition work? Do women also present their own phalli?'

'Yes, they could. I have about eight to ten different phalli with me, which were offered by different women. They are in different shapes and sizes, most of which are made from wood. Some don't even look like penises but are still blessed with the power of the saint. How it works is that these women come and present the phallus to the *malang* here. The *malang's* wife then takes the woman to a separate room where she rubs the phallus on her stomach and she becomes impregnated. I can't tell you the things I have seen with my own eyes. Women who are too old to have children have walked out from here bearing a child.'

I wondered if this was the 'immoral' activity that Akhtar was talking about at the previous shrine. Was the rubbing over the stomach a euphemism? If Hajra too was impregnating women in this way which perhaps the elderly of the village perceived as an act of sexual libertinism, which it was clearly not meant to be.

It looks as if the backlash and the propaganda against

their tradition have also affected the way they look at their own beliefs. Towards the end of the conversation, Faheem got a bit apologetic when he said, 'The magic is not in the penis. It is in the blessing of the saint. The saint in this case has blessed these wooden penises. If you go to the shrine of Baba Lal Hassan [which is only a few kilometres from here] you will find that the log of a tree there is blessed. People come and rub their bruises and body parts with the log and get cured. It is only because of the power of the saint not because of the object.'

'Do you know that there is another shrine of phallic offerings also referred to as Aban Shah near Pakpattan?' I asked Faheem.

'Really? I didn't know that. I know that there is another shrine near Barbegi Katalpur near Abdul Hakeem. Actually that's not really a shrine. It was the *dhoan*[17] of the saint. He spent some time there and eventually a shrine was built to commemorate the spot. I have been there a couple of times.'

'Do they also have phallic offerings?' I asked him.

'No, they don't. Maybe the shrine that you are talking about was another *dhoan* of the saint. I'll check it out soon.'

The story narrated by Hanifa, which had sounded irrelevant, now made sense. Her brother had known that this was the real shrine of Aban Shah whereas the other one was only his *dhoan*. However, I still doubt that Aban Shah was his real name even though his descendant Faheem claims it is. I believe it was a title bestowed on him because of his blessings. To be honest, I am not even sure if there was a person or a saint who started this tradition, at least not 350 years ago. This is an ancient tradition.

For the generation of Pakistanis who were born after the creation of this country, this syncretism of different religions became an anomaly, which defied their nationalism. In order to justify that irregularity, sometimes Muslim saints and such legendary stories were invented to justify devotion to a 'non-Muslim' tradition. Aban Shah sounded to me like an ancient cult and a figure that was resurrected to fit within the framework of a newly created Islamic country. However, it now seems the legend and the tradition need another revision as the practices are facing criticism from those who espouse the puritanical versions of Islam. Just like Partition once altered the way this religious practice was perceived, a rise in 'pure' Islam would also have to be accommodated accordingly.

# 3

## Sacred Trees

I WAS EAGER TO see the sacred log that Syed Faheem Abbas had referred to during our conversation.

'It's nothing special, just a log lying in the middle of the field with people praying around it. Let's go home instead and have tea,' said Altaf.

For him this was an ordinary scene, which one gets accustomed to if one has grown up in that environment. However, for me, behind this ordinary practice lay an extraordinary historical continuation. These acts are ordinary for the locals primarily because they are the continuation of traditions developed thousands of years ago. Their drabness accumulated over generations was the reason they were so fascinating for me. I had heard the Indian civilization was the oldest living civilization in the world and here it was in front of me, centuries unfolding as if nothing had changed.

Nauman was fasting which meant that we had to wrap up before sunset. The sky had transformed into a burning pink, soon to fade out, making way for the encroaching darkness.

Standing in the middle of an empty field was a newly constructed tomb of the saint, a single-storey building waiting for a paint job. A group of old men sat nearby playing cards. Gambling is illegal in the country, even if done in the privacy of one's home. It was banned in the late seventies as then prime minister, Zulfikar Ali Bhutto, a self-confessed 'Islamic' socialist, struggled to hold onto power in the face of the massive onslaught from the opposition. Banning gambling along with alcohol was his gambit to cater to the Islamic religiosity of the people. And yet gambling and the consumption of alcohol continues unhindered in every nook and corner of Pakistan, in the form of money hidden underneath a mat during a game of cards, or vodka carried in mineral water bottles. The men playing cards were too engrossed in their game of high stakes and ignored us arriving in a car, a rare sight at this shrine. However, for a group of child musicians sitting on a log facing the side entrance of the tomb, our arrival in a car promised rewards. They clapped, played their instruments and danced in the hope of some small change, a fortune for them.

The sacred log rested in the middle of a piece of vacant land spared from the vegetation. The ground below the log was covered with bricks, arbitrarily put together to differentiate the sacred space from the rest of the ground. The log was covered with a green cloth, usually used to cover the graves of saints as a mark of respect. The colour green, which is said to be the favourite of the Prophet of Islam, is now universally accepted as the colour of Islam. Parts uncovered by the cloth were blackened due to weathering. A few burned-out lamps were placed under the trunk to be used for religious rituals.

We were accompanied by two locals who were immediately

recognized. Everyone is a distant relative in a village, their origin usually associated with a particular fraternity group. The growth of villages is a result of the growth of that particular family. The thirty-seven-year-old Imaad Hussain Shah, the current guardian of the shrine, who drew his lineage from that of the saint interred here, was introduced to me by Nauman. He wore a turban and a shalwar kameez. His golden ring and watch glimmered in the fading light of the sun. Like Faheem, he had benefitted from his spiritual caste. He had striking features, hazel eyes and a neat red moustache, and stood with a dignified posture, folding his hands in front while talking in a low volume, uncharacteristic of Punjabis.

'I am from the ninth generation of the saint. Baba Lal Hassan [the occupant of the grave] came to this place from a village in Tehsil Shourkot, Jang [about seventy-five kilometres from here]. After the death of his father, his stepbrothers refused to give him his legitimate share of his father's property. In anger, the saint cursed the land and cast a spell over the animals as a result of which the land became barren and the animals refused to work. Having realized the reason for this curse, they asked for forgiveness and returned the rightful property to the saint. However, Baba Lal Hassan did not do this for his share in the property. He just wanted to teach his brothers a lesson. He took the property and distributed it between his stepsisters. Then when he decided to leave the village, his brother exhorted him to stay but he didn't listen.'

While Imaad narrated the story, an old man, about seventy years old and wearing a kurta and dhoti, approached the trunk. He bowed down touching the lower end of the log with his forehead and stayed in that posture for a little while. Noticing my interest in the visitor, Imaad stopped narrating the story and allowed me to photograph the scene. When the old man stood up, he prayed standing in front of the tree and then left, oblivious to my curiosity about him.

'After walking for some time, the saint stopped under the shade of a *kikkar* [acacia], which is this particular tree. There were also a few women sitting nearby. The saint asked them for water but they thought the saint was flirting with them, so they refused to serve him water and asked him to leave. The saint replied that he wanted to stand for a while under the shade. "Take your tree with you," the girls mocked him. "So be it," he replied. He sat on his horse and began to ride away and the tree followed, providing him with shade throughout the journey. Finally when the saint got to this place, the tree rested at this particular spot and has been here ever since.'

At one end of the tree, there were three branches protruding outwards. I imagined the tree walking with these branches. Or maybe the story of the walking tree developed because the tree had branches that looked like legs.

'How old is this story?' I asked Imaad.

'This happened about 300 years ago. My father and grandfather have all reported to have seen this tree in this very condition since they were children. It hasn't even weathered with time whereas a normal tree would have.'

Needless to say I have always been sceptical of stories involving the miracles of saints. Firstly, they are passed down orally through generations as a result of which the story takes on a life of its own, feeding off the people's imaginations. Over generations the feats of the forefathers become even grander and their negative aspects even more irrelevant.

This has sadly been the case with all religious personalities. They are raised to superhuman levels, which damages the entire purpose of religiosity. I have always argued that if these individuals were allowed to remain human, which they essentially were, their feats of tolerance, fearlessness and opposition in the face of persecution would become even more extraordinary and a greater inspiration for ordinary people. When raised to metaphysical levels, the achievements of these individuals end up being attributed to divine favour and thus they become more out of reach of the ordinary. My second reason for doubting the authenticity of this saint was the political motivation of Imaad and his family. He claimed to draw direct lineage from the saint, which meant that he also received all the favours which accrued as a result of being heir to the shrine, including respect, honour, gifts and other monetary advantages. I believe that like the shrines of Aban Shah, this too must have been an ancient shrine, dedicated to the acacia tree which later became associated with the saint Baba Lal Hassan. The story must have been created by his followers. The tree worship would have already existed here when Baba Lal Hassan arrived. After his death he would have been interred here and the story constructed.

Ancient traditions which link back to the Indus Valley Civilization support my thesis. Trees have been worshipped for thousands of years in this region. Seals depicting sacred trees have been discovered by archaeologists from the ruins of Indus Valley Civilization. Along with peepal tree, the acacia tree, which is worshipped at this particular shrine, is most frequently depicted. Animals and mysterious creatures have been featured with the trees on these seals, which archaeologists believe to have been inserted as protective forces. Swastika, a significant symbol in Hindu iconography, has also been associated with acacia trees in these seals.[18] In his book *The Tree of Life: An Archaeological Study*, Edwin Oliver James notes:

> From the Indus seals and amulets the peepal and the acacia appear to have been the most venerated trees, the former having remained an object of universal worship in India, and as the abode of the Hindu Triad, Brahma, Vishnu and Shiva, it became peculiarly sacred equated with the highest concept of deity in Hinduism and so deeply laid in the ancient Indus valley civilization. It was worshipped by pouring waters on its roots, making votive offerings to it by tying rags on its branches (something that is still practiced in Muslim Pakistan) and applying red ochre as the surrogate of the blood to its trunk.[19]

William Henry Sleeman, a well-known British official in India from the early nineteenth century, while recording the religious rituals of Hindus, notes the following in his book, *Rambles and Recollections of an Indian Official*:

> When Ram set out with his army for Ceylon, he is supposed to have worshipped the little tree called 'cheonkul', which stood near his capital of Ajodhya. It is a wretched little thing between a shrub and a tree; but I have seen a procession of more than seventy thousands persons attend their prince to the worship of it on the festival of the Dashara, which is held

in the celebration of this expedition to Ceylon. As Arjuna and his brothers worshipped the shumee-tree, the *Acacia suma*, and hung up their arms upon it, so the Hindus go forth to worship that tree on the festival of the Dashara. They address the tree with the name Aparajita, the invincible goddess, and sprinkle it with five ambrosial liquids, wash it with water and hang garments upon it. They light lamps and burn incense before the symbol of Aparajita, make 'chandlos' upon the tree, sprinkle it with rose-colored offerings and set offerings of food before it.[20]

The sacredness of the acacia tree is deeply ingrained in the religious psyche of the people of South Asia, including Buddhists. It is believed that Khadiravani Tara or 'the Tara of the acacia forest'[21] who is a Buddhist goddess known to offer shelter, nourishment and healing, derives her visual iconography from the tree of acacia, with which she is associated, as the tree is hardwood fruit-bearing with medicinal properties.[22]

The acacia tree reappears in the Punjabi folk love legend of Mirza-Sahiban highlighting its significance in Punjabi culture. The death of the protagonist takes place under this tree. The symbolism associated with this tree can also be found in the poetry of the mystic Punjabi Sufi poet of the mid-nineteenth century, Mian Muhammad Baksh.

Interestingly, the acacia tree was also worshipped in the pagan religious practices of Arabia before the origin of Islam, part of which seeped into the new religion. However, in the Arabia of today, which is dominated by the Wahhabi school of thought, which vehemently opposes folk religious practices, these traditions now only exist in books and historical records, unlike in Pakistan where they are still alive and thriving.

William Gifford Palgrave, a nineteenth-century scholar from Britain, was an anthropologist and an expert on Arabian culture. Travelling through Arabia in 1862-63, he noted a unique ritual based around an acacia tree, in which devotees would dance around it praying for rain. These were Muslims who had maintained certain pagan beliefs and customs, he observed.[23]

While we were still standing with Imaad, a group of women approached the tree and took off their shoes before stepping on the bricks where the sacred log rested. One of the women was wearing a burqa. As the other women stood at a little distance from the log, the woman with the burqa bent and kissed the trunk as if it was a beloved object. The group left after offering their prayers.

The pink of the sky was completely consumed by grey. We could hear the loud chirping of birds returning to their nests. Anytime now the muezzin would echo the sound of Azaan marking the end of the fast for the day. We headed back to Nauman's house just in time to break the fast.

'You know that tree wasn't an acacia tree,' said Iqbal Qaiser as he gulped down tea along with pakoras. 'It was shisham.'

≈

I couldn't grasp the extent of its size from the outside. Initially I was disappointed as the banyan tree that I had heard so much about looked rather small. But in reality, the tree that was situated in the middle of a field turned out to be a never-ending labyrinth of branches. The solo tree was a forest all by itself. There were a few houses around it, lone houses constructed in the openness of the field.

If placed in a mythical novel, the banyan tree would be an antagonist because of the way it expands. But it happens to be one of the most sacred trees of South Asia, sacred in literally all religious traditions. From its branches it has rope-like structures called bough that fall towards the ground. Upon touching the ground they enter the surface and over time solidify into branches with boughs hanging from them. In this way, feeding off the ground, the tree continues expanding as the younger branches replace the old ones. For this particular quality, the banyan tree is considered immortal.[24]

In the case of the tree standing in front of us, it seemed as if the younger branches had consumed the original tree. There was no centre and branches shapelessly extended in different directions. In the middle of the tree, enclosed by branches, was a small platform made of bricks, perhaps for sitting. Numerous graves covered with green cloths were scattered around it, one of which was the grave of the saint. On the branches of what appeared to be the main trunk of the tree, pieces of cloth, mostly green, had been tied as a supplication.

Surrounding us were tourists from neighbouring areas, who on their arrival almost ritualistically offered prayers to the graves here. Engraved with a knife were names of some of these visitors, eager to leave a permanent mark on history. A few had also left their mobile numbers, probably hoping to initiate a secret love affair in this highly monitored social life of rural Punjab.

This banyan tree was located in the outskirts of a small

village called Apal Muri near my ancestral village of Jalap, district Sargodha. It has been an annual family tradition for us to visit my paternal grandparents here on the second day of Eid. According to the Mirasi of the village, a caste that traditionally maintained the family trees of all important families, this small village on the banks of the river Chenab was founded by my great great grandfather, Ahmad Elahi. Better educated than the rest of the rural folk around him, he became a quack. Till recently a part of the family continued to practise 'medicine' in the village. Only when a government hospital was established in a neighbouring village did their practice fade away.

Ahmad Elahi was originally named Ghasita Ram, a Hindu, who converted to Islam at the age of seventeen. He moved to this area from the Jhelum sometime in the late nineteenth century, abandoning his family who disapproved of him opting out of their religion. There is no written evidence explaining his motivation for conversion, but according to oral testimonies of the Mirasi, Ghasita Ram converted to marry a Muslim girl. I have always wondered what would have happened had he not fallen in love with her. Would my ancestors have been massacred at the time of Partition or would they have safely made it to India? It also fascinates me that he opted to settle on the banks of this particular river. The Chenab, in the folk culture of Punjab, is known as the river of love. The celebrated folk love legend of Sohni and Mahiwal unfolded around this river, finally drowning a distraught Sohni as she attempted to swim across the river to meet her beloved, settled on the other side. Takth Hazara, the ancestral village of Ranjha, protagonist of the love legend

Heer-Ranjha is also next to the Chenab, a few kilometres away from our village. Was Ghasita Ram aware of this connection between the Chenab and love when he settled here?

≈

For some time now my father, from whom I have inherited a love for the study of history and culture, had wanted to show me this ancient banyan tree. So, on this particular Eid we headed out to Apal Muri which is at a little distance from Jalap, next to Takht Hazara.

As I stood under the tree, as if caged on all sides, photographing the intricate patterns of branches, an old woman approached me. Whereas social concerns in cities would not allow a woman, even if old to talk to a strange man, here in rural areas these modicums of civilization didn't apply.

'This tree was laid by the saint who is now buried under it. He had a long life, several hundreds of years. People in the old days used to have long lives. When the tree grew big he used to sit underneath it and pray,' she told me.

I learned later her name was Munawar Begum.

'How long ago was that?' I asked.

'A long time ago, too long ago to remember!'

'Who are these other people buried around him?'

'These are all devotees of the saint, people who loved him.'

Munawar Begum lived in the house next to the tree. Branches of the tree overshadowed the courtyard of her house but her family refused to cut it.

'Djinns live in the tree. They are all pious, Muslims. Hindu djinns are evil. But if we cut any part of the tree they will get angry and will occupy our houses. The djinns can take various forms. Often at night we hear them as sheep, sometimes also as humans, but we don't get scared because we know they won't harm us. They will harm us only if we bother them. Sometimes our cows and buffaloes make strange noises at night because of the djinns.'

The djinns that Munawar Begum referred to are *yakshas*, ancient Hindu tree spirits. The belief that the banyan tree is occupied by good-natured spirits or djinns comes from ancient beliefs codified in Hinduism. In ancient India, along with local deities people worshipped trees, lakes, animals, etc. One of the most well-known spirits associated with the worship of trees was Yaksha, believed to reside on the branches and in the roots of banyan trees.[25] As Hinduism developed into its modern version, such folk religious practices also found their way into Brahmanism. In the Bhagavad Gita, the book of ethics of Hinduism, Lord Krishna states that the banyan tree is his embodiment out of all the trees. It is referred to as the abode of all the spirits, according to the scripture Atharva Veda. Worship of the banyan tree is also believed to cure leprosy, bring progeny and remove bad omen.[26]

Banyan trees are known as 'bodh' in Punjabi, a name that they borrow from Buddhism. In Buddhist literature, the banyan tree is referred to as the bodhi tree, or the tree of enlightenment as it is believed that Lord Buddha received his enlightenment under a banyan tree. It is also believed that during his meditation, when the demon Sujata came to distract him, the guardian spirit of the tree came down to protect him. Falling leaves from the trees and sagging boughs, subsequently, became symbols of the guardian spirit.

It is clear that this quaint religious tradition upheld by the people of this village and neighbouring areas is not a peripheral religious practice but rather a sophisticated religious tradition that has developed over centuries, bequeathed to them orally by their ancestors. Today the origin of the practice has become irrelevant. The tradition developed over thousands of years has become too strong to be disowned as mere superstition. It provides them with a reason to continue the worship of the banyan tree without worrying about its 'un-Islamic-ness'.

'This tree is now dying,' said a friend of my father, who was accompanying us. He also belonged to Jalap. 'The last time I came here it was much bigger. I think the locals have started cutting the branches that encroach on their house. They don't believe in the spirit stories anymore. A few years ago, some representatives from the Geological Department measured the circumference of the tree. They calculated it to be spread over an area of four acres. As it stands right now, I think only about three acres are left.'

Perhaps the younger generation has stopped believing in the stories of djinns.

Back in Lahore, I approached my friend Salman Rashid, a well-known travel writer, with pictures of the tree, almost certain that he would add to my knowledge about it. Sitting in his sun-lit study, Salman Rashid marvelled at the pictures of this gigantic tree. In a rural environment, Muslim or Hindu, a tree this size was inevitably linked to mythical creatures.

'I have heard of a bodhi tree in Islamabad and one near Jhelum but I had no idea that there was another one. Where is this again?' he asked me.

'There is a book which allegedly contains the letters of Alexander the Great, written to his philosopher teacher

Aristotle. These weren't written by Alexander himself as there is evidence to prove that they were written after his death. However, they do make for an interesting read. In one such letter, Alexander says that an old Indian man visited him in Jhelum after his war with Porus, and told him of two talking trees, one male and the other female at a little distance from Jhelum. The letter states that Alexander then visited the trees and indeed found them to be talking to each other. Given the standards of those times, Sargodha was not very far from Jhelum. Do you think one of those talking tree is this one? The sound of the leaves in a gentle breeze would have given the effect of someone whispering.' I narrated to Salman Rashid the story told to me by Munawar Begum.

'Absolutely rubbish. Look closely. Where there should be the mother trunk of the tree is now only its branches, which means that the original tree is dead. The main trunk of a banyan tree can live up to 2,000 years. If the original trunk is dead then I'll say that this tree is at least 2,000 years old. But who knows how long ago the main trunk died. This could be 2,500 as well or maybe even older. There was no Islam at that time so how could there be a Muslim saint?'

The story developed in my head. Like other shrines this one also would have converted after Partition. The grave could have been a samadhi or an idol, or any other object of worship which was changed to cater to a changing religious sensibility. The tree became a Muslim banyan tree.

≈

# 4

## Into the Heart of Orthodoxy

WHEN I FIRST heard about Mussadiq I imagined an old man, someone in his early fifties with white hair and a serene face. However, when I saw him I was surprised to discover that he was almost as old as me, in his early twenties. (Mussadiq was supposed to take me to Raiwind, the heart of Islamic orthodoxy in Pakistan. It was therefore obvious that he was a religious man and in my head religion was associated with older people.) Wearing a kurta and a skull cap, he had a long beard with no moustache, typical of Muslims. His shalwar was raised till his ankles, a distinctive feature of his 'school of thought'.

He came out of his house, a spacious double-storey structure located in the heart of Defence Housing Authority (DHA, Lahore) considered to be the elitist locality in the city, accompanied by a friend of the same age and with a similar appearance. His friend parked his bicycle in the garage while Mussadiq took out his car, a Suzuki Cultus. Mussadiq appeared to belong to the upper-middle class, while his friend seemed to be from the lower class. However, as they prepared to take me to the centre of Tableeghi Jamaat in Raiwind, their economic and social differences were obliterated and they talked to each other candidly, as close friends.

A post-colonial state, Pakistan takes pride in its Victorian code of ethics in which different economic and social classes are kept apart. I also have friends who belong to the same socio-economic class as me. On the couple of occasions when I have sensed a potential bond with someone from a much lower class than mine, my inherent inhibition has prevented me from exploring the opportunity. Although I realize this is a shortcoming, I continue to be choosy in my selection of friends. But here were two friends who belonged to two distinct worlds coming together by the force of religion to become close friends. Whatever bias I had was beginning to fade away.

Mussadiq works with his father who owns a car spare-parts shop on McLeod Road. This is a multi-million rupee business. His friend Akhtar, on the other hand, is the son of a maulvi of a mosque in DHA and is waiting to take up his position after his father's retirement. Mussadiq happens to be a graduate in Business Studies from one of the leading educational institutes of the city whereas Akhtar has only completed his matriculation. The two met for the first time in Raiwind, about an hour's journey away. The Tableeghi Jamaat in Pakistan has its headquarters in Raiwind.

The Tableeghi Jamaat, the preaching assembly, was founded in 1927 by a man called Muhammad Ilyas with its centre in New Delhi, where it still remains. He was a Muslim scholar inspired by the Deobandi school of thought (Deobandi promotes a literalist interpretation of Islam derived from the Quran and the Hadith of the Prophet of Islam. It looks down upon shrine culture, regarding it as a corruption of pure religion intermingled with Hindu tradition). He worked in undivided rural Punjab, exhorting Muslims to 'purify' their religious practices which he argued were corrupted due to the influence of the dominant Hindu culture.[27] The movement which has now become a global phenomenon with centres all over the world, originated at the height of the Hindu-Muslim rivalry of the early twentieth century in northern India. In Pakistani context, the creation of the country is the end product of this inter-religious rivalry. Ironically when Pakistan was created, the head of the Tableeghi Jamaat at that time, Muhammad Ilyas' son, refused to migrate to the new country and continued living in New Delhi. In the subsequent years, Raiwind, a small village in the outskirts of Lahore, emerged as one of the leading centres of the movement in the world. The annual gathering of Muslims here is estimated to be the second largest in the world after the Hajj congregation in Mecca, attracting about two million people from all parts of the country and abroad.[28]

The early twentieth century in British India was the time when European rationalism and theories of enlightenment had seeped into the elite of the colonial state as a result of which religious preachers and leaders re-interpreted their religious theories to incorporate modern values. One such movement inspired by European rationalism was the Arya Samaj, founded in the late nineteenth century. This was a Hindu reformist movement centred on the authority of the holy books of Vedas. The leading protagonists of the movement were alarmed by the success of the Christian missionaries in converting Hindu untouchables to Christianity. In order to woo them back, as well as other non-Hindus who were seen as former Hindus, they initiated a movement called Shuddhi which meant purity or purification. This was a movement targeted to bring back untouchables and non-Hindus into the fold of Vedic traditions.[29]

Muslim reformists like Muhammad Ilyas who were alarmed by the Shuddhi Movement founded reformist movements of their own, aggravating the communal tension in Punjab. The movement forbade the proselytizing of non-Muslims and instead provided the renewal of Islamic faith to existent Muslims,[30] a policy they have continued to adhere to. The movement found particular success in the urban centres attracting cadres from petty bourgeoisie (tradesman, junior civil servants, etc.) and wealthier social circles (liberal professionals, businessmen, etc.).[31] Vehemently opposed to folk Islam, a few aspects of which are discussed in the earlier sections of the book, preachers of the movement focus on southern Punjab and rural Sindh where syncretistic religion held sway. Centred on the concept of preaching Islam, the Tableeghi Jamaat strictly refrains from political matters and controversial debates on Islamic jurisprudence.

I was introduced to Mussadiq by a college mate who was working with me on a class presentation on the Tableeghi Jamaat. Driving towards Raiwind, Mussadiq explained to me the concept of the preaching movement.

'To preach Islam is Sunnah [practices of the Prophet of Islam emulated by Muslims in their quest to be the perfect human being that he was]. There is no other better way to spend one's life than to spread the message of Allah and his Prophet, peace be upon him. There is still so much *jahalliya* in Pakistan [*jahalliya* is an Arabic word that means ignorance. Used in the Islamic context it connotes divine ignorance, an ignoble state]. There are several shrines in the Multan region and in Sindh where people still practise Hinduism and give it the name of Islam. They are influenced by Hindu culture. They light lamps, present offerings to the shrine and even bow down to the grave, an act of *shirk* [comparing an entity with Allah, an act of blasphemy]. Parties from the Tableeghi Jamaat regularly travel all over the country teaching such Muslims the true meaning of Islam. Devotees volunteer for parties and bear their own expenses. They carry minimum luggage and spend nights at the local mosques. Those who can afford it even go abroad. Our parties have travelled as far as Africa, United States, Australia and China.'

The Tableeghi Jamaat centre in Raiwind was spread over several acres. Near its entrance was a huge vacant ground and next to it was a room meant to facilitate preachers from other cities and countries. The langar hall or the community kitchen was also next to the parking lot.

The main hall where the congregation gathers for lessons on Islamic faith was huge, divided into three floors with a basement where construction work was underway. Speakers had been placed all over the halls to broadcast the message of the preacher sitting on a pulpit near the entrance. This was where Mussadiq led us. There was a strange serene atmosphere all around the centre. The people were particularly polite and spoke in low volumes. Even the volume of the speakers was maintained such that the sound was audible, not loud. This was in contrast to the way loudspeakers at mosques blast fiery sermons of the maulvis on auspicious days. Scattered all over the halls were devotees who had come to renew their faith. Some were offering prayers, while others slept. This was an all male gathering. I was told there was a separate section for females. Interaction between the two was not allowed. Mussadiq planned to spend two nights at the centre and return after the weekend. He told me that he usually comes here on weekends in search of peace.

Behind the halls was the madrassah for students of religion. This too was divided into two sections, one for the locals and the other for international students. As I roamed around this area trying to find an international student to talk to, I saw several children of different nationalities: Chinese, Southeast Asians, Afghanis, Central Asians, Africans and even Europeans. Eager to help me out, one of the local students who seemed to have a particular fascination for me, introduced me to an Australian student living at the seminary.

Ismael, who couldn't speak Urdu, talked about how his family opposed his idea of moving to Pakistan to study religion. 'In the end I just moved here without their consent. I haven't been in touch with them for the past two years, ever since I moved here.'

'What motivated you to study Islam?' I asked him.

'I realized that the life I was living was too materialistic and shallow. There was always something missing. There always will be if you don't follow religion. Brother, you should explore Islam. It's a beautiful religion.'

Since the students are trained in preaching, inevitably every conversation at Tableeghi Jamaat ends up being a preaching of Islam.

'How was your life in Australia before you moved here?' I asked.

'I don't want to talk about it,' Ismael replied.

'How come?'

'Brother, if you don't stop asking me about my past I will have to get up and leave.'

'Sorry! Please don't do that.'

According to Islamic tradition, once a life of *jahalliya* has been abandoned and the right path of Islam adopted, one should not talk about the *jahalliya* days. This applies to the individual and the community. Once the Prophet of Islam gained control over Kaaba in Mecca, the holiest shrine for the Muslims but also considered holy in pagan Arabia, he removed all the idols in a symbolic act that was meant to clearly demarcate the past from the present. There was no need to talk about the time of *jahalliya* anymore, a time before Islam. However, history, one of the prime sources of identity for human existence, cannot be shunned away as easily therefore it was recast to serve a particular agenda of explaining the rise of Islam. All the ancient civilizations like the Egyptian, Babylonian, Byzantine and the Roman were studied in this new paradigm—their eventual downfall explained by their rejection of God.

In Pakistan, if one ever goes to visit Harappa and Mohenjo-daro one would notice that the locals swarm around tourists offering their services as guides. Almost without exception, these amateur guides cite the wrath of God as the reason for the destruction of these ancient cities. Various religious-political leaders have argued that Pakistanis should once again fill the excavated sites of their ruins and disassociate with anything that relates to the era of *jahalliya*.

I remember once visiting my friend's parents after their arrival from Hajj to congratulate them. When the father learned that I have a passion for history he told me that I should stop reading all history books and should only read the Quran as 'it contains all the history that I ever need to know'. Similarly on another occasion, when I was petitioning with a group of prominent architects from the city to save the destruction of a historic Hindu temple in Lahore that was being encroached upon by the local populace, one of the architects approached me and asked if it was un-Islamic to save a Hindu temple, giving me the example of the conquest of Mecca and the destruction of all the idols there by the Prophet himself. Intrigued I approached one of my Islamic teachers at university, a charismatic young man. With immaculate English and rhetorical charisma, he has managed to Islamize several young students at my liberal university to the chagrin of the left-leaning professors. I asked him if he thought that the science of archaeology was 'un-Islamic'.

'The question is not if it is un-Islamic or not. The question is about priorities. It pains me to read that UNESCO has reserved two million dollars for the renovation of a major archaeological site, and on the next page of the magazine there is an article on children dying of hunger.'

Poignant though the reply was, it didn't answer my question.

Heading out of the madrassah, I ran into a few students from Uzbekistan. While laughing and joking with me, they told me that they had come via Afghanistan. When I asked them if they had been through the proper immigration process, they laughed at my naivety, and refused to answer.

It is here that I also met a European student from Macedonia. Abraham was about twenty-five years old and particularly good-looking with blue eyes. His reasons for coming to Pakistan were similar to those of Ismael—that of trying to fill the void created by a materialistically oriented world.

'Pray for my brother,' he urged me. 'He is still a party animal and doesn't listen to anyone.'

Leaving the comforts of their homes, these students, some of whom are only children, spend several years in these hostels, living with the most basic facilities and are completely cut off from the rest of the world. Several don't return until they complete the entire syllabus. Their bedding is nothing but straw mats and their classroom is a huge hall, where sitting with one knee clasped and the other resting on the ground they oscillate, remembering their lessons of the day, which begin as early as dawn and end at night. Later in the morning and in the afternoon, they are allowed a few hours of rest. Older students are permitted to venture into the village.

'What do you want to do after you graduate from here?' I asked Abraham.

'I might go back to Macedonia for a little while to meet my family after which I would spend my entire life preaching the word of Allah. I would travel to every nook and corner of the world with His word and usher people into a world of enlightenment.'

Upon graduating, most of the students continue living the spartan life.

Mussadiq wanted me to have dinner at the langar hall before I left, so I accompanied him and his friends to the hall. We climbed to the first floor of the newly constructed hall where Pakistani students from the madrassah served the guests. They brought Mussadiq a huge plate filled with *alu gosht* (meat and potatoes), served with a few rotis. Mussadiq told me this was all we were going to get for dinner and asked me to join in. According to the tradition here, no one is served a separate plate but is expected to eat from a communal serving.

'This adds *barkat* [blessing] to the food. It is the Sunnah of the Prophet (PBUH), the beloved.'

Despite being conscious about hygiene, I was humbled by the experience. I seized to be an individual and became part of a community.

In a post-industrial world where the sole focus of existence is the advancement of the self and accumulation of wealth, the reassurance provided by the feeling of belonging to a group was liberating. This is what must attract so many young people towards religion.

'After 9/11 when there was a crackdown on all the religious seminaries of the country, didn't the seminary here attract the attention of the authorities?' I asked Mussadiq.

'The government cannot dare to do anything here. We are an apolitical entity but we are powerful,' he said, chuckling.

Over the years the Tableeghi Jamaat has made inroads into the social fabric of the country with several popular celebrities, politicians, bureaucrats and businessmen drawn into its network. A few years ago, a leading cricketer of the country, Saeed Anwar, was inspired by the Tableeghi Jamaat and turned religious. The rest of the team followed him. The cricketers included Inzamam-ul-Haq, Mushtaq Ahmed, Saqlain Mushtaq. Yousuf Youhana, the only Christian in the national team at that time, converted to Islam and became Muhammad Yousuf. Another celebrity-turned-Tableeghi is Junaid Jamshed, a leading Pakistani singer. Now he only sings hymns in praise of the Prophet of Islam.

At the centre, Junaid Jamshed's conversion is viewed as a source of pride, and his name often comes up in conversation. 'If having sinned for so long [most of the devotees here regard music to be un-Islamic] Junaid Jamshed can turn to the true path then there is hope for you too,' the elderly tell young devotees.

'You should come during the *ijtima* [the annual congregation],' advised Mussadiq. 'Then you will understand the true strength of the Tableeghi Jamaat.'

Even though I never returned to the annual congregation held in November, I have a fair idea of what the event is like. Every year, traffic routes are directed to cater to the multitudes of pilgrims who come packed in overflowing buses especially booked for them. Thousands of cars laden with luggage also head towards Raiwind, causing a major traffic jam at one of the junctions I regularly use.

One of my uncles also happens to be an ardent follower of the Tableeghi Jamaat and ever since his 'conversion', he has been regularly attending the congregation. Only a few years ago he was settled in Bangkok where he had a successful hotel business. A very talented person, he had a knack for music and would sing for hours at family gatherings, often after downing a couple of drinks. However, a few years ago, inspired by religious preaching, he grew a beard, gave up drinking and stopped listening to music. His family initially objected to this transformation, protesting every time he would disappear for weeks to preach, but now they have got used to it.

The Tableeghi Jamaat has managed to permeate the social fabric of the major cities of Punjab, taking people away from the world of materialism and bringing them to the world of religion. With this conversion from materialism to religion gaining ground, shrines similar to the ones at Kamalia and Apal Muri are likely to face a major onslaught due to their 'impure' religious practices, in coming years.

Stepping out of the langar hall, I saw a fascinating scene. Hundreds of young boys had gathered in pairs and were facing each other. While one unleashed a didactic parade of words, the other listened patiently. It was fast and sounded rehearsed. I stood next to a pair of boys but the speaker ignored me.

'What are they doing?' I asked Mussadiq.

'They're performing *zikr*, the remembrance of Allah. Every night after dinner all the students of the seminary gather in pairs. One of them talks about any religious matter while the other listens. When the speaker finishes it is the turn of the listener to speak.'

The entire courtyard was filled with the droning sound of hundreds of boys talking in a monotonic manner.

'This is also a Sunnah,' said Mussadiq.

≈

# 5

## A Mutiny from within

JUST AS I was about to enter Hardee's, a multinational fast food chain, my photographer friend Rida Arif called me to say she was waiting inside. She ordered her meal and sat opposite me while I buried myself in my diary trying to find something to do as we waited for Anam and Iqbal Qaiser to join us.

This particular branch of Hardee's had opened recently, after the fast food chain's initial success in Lahore. There was a KFC at the service station next door. Ever since the construction of the motorway that connects Lahore to Islamabad and Peshawar, Thokhar Niaz Baig has transformed from an obscure locality to a happening place, with people scrambling to set up new service stations and fast-food outlets here. I could hear American hip-hop music playing in the background, while at the table facing me, a group of young boys watched an English Premier League football match on the plasma television.

'This is a different world altogether, different from the one we are heading down to,' I wrote in my diary. 'For most of the people sitting around us—educated people from English-medium schools—the city of Chunian where the festival is, doesn't even exist. In fact they might even struggle to identify any city that the pilgrims there came from—Habibullah, Arifwala, etc. Yet both these worlds exist, separated by years of disconnect. It feels like we are going to a place which is out of context in this globalized-industrialized world. That world consists of superstition, magic and miracles. But then I wonder if the shrine is out of context, or is it the bubble that we occupy in the urban centres that is out of context in the culture of Punjab. The question comes down to whose context.'

'Can you please open this for me?' I looked up to see Rida holding onto a sachet of ketchup struggling to cut through it with her sticky hands. After trying in vain, I gestured to a waiter to help us out.

'What are you writing?' Rida asked me.

'You can read it if you want to.'

'Our waiter is a dark-skinned Christian boy named Samson. He lives at Niaz Baig along with his brother whereas his family originally belongs to the city of Muridke. His dark skin is a legacy of the thousands of years his ancestors have spent working in the sun as Hindu untouchables. In order to escape the stigma they must have converted to Christianity in the late twentieth century, with the advent of the British. Once upon a time, even the presence of his shadow would have tainted our food. In some areas, in the land of magic and miracles, a remnant of that tradition of discrimination still exists. But here, in a multinational fast food chain, which heralds the arrival of globalization, he opens the sachet with his bare hands. Not all is bad with the globalization of values and not all is good with keeping of culture and traditions.'

From the Multan Road highway we took a left entering into the infamous forests of Changa Manga. It was already dark so there was a sense of fear in the car. Changa Manga has a history of notoriety especially with regard to pilgrims at night. At least till a few years ago, no one dared to pass through this forest at night because of the dacoits who inhabited it. It is much safer now, since the Punjab government introduced the motorway police. Even though this secluded single-lane road doesn't fall under their jurisdiction, its proximity to the national highway ensures its security.

The police jeeps patrolling the road made us feel safe yet we were of the fact that an element of danger still lurked behind the camouflage of the forest. While I was driving, Iqbal Qaiser, sitting next to me was conspicuously quiet, aware of the invisible threat that travelling on this road at night presented. A couple of years ago, before the administrative changes at the Punjab Cultural Institute put an untimely end to his project, Iqbal Qaiser was working on an encyclopedia of Lahore, the first of its kind. Divided into five different parts, each about 1,000 pages, he spent years studying land revenue records and digging through government archives, sifting through the history of several villages in and around the district of Lahore. Till 1972, Chunian district was part of Lahore and he had gone through the land revenue records of Changa Manga for his project.

'According to the records at the Forest Department, Changa Manga has always been a natural jungle. However, during the British era, in order to rein in the outlaws who would take refuge in its depth, the government created a natural forest here, and used its wood to fuel the railways. Later when coal-run engines were introduced, they started using the wood for furniture and also experimented with silkworm farming here, which surprisingly did well. The forest project officially began in 1866. In 1960, the Pakistan government gave it the status of a national park,' he had narrated to me a few years ago while I was researching on the historic villages, towns and cities on Multan Road.

'The name of Changa Manga comes from two dacoits who escaped from prison and found shelter here, and started harassing travellers. This was during the British era. Later when they were killed in an encounter, this forest was named after them. However, there is a reason to believe that this is an apocryphal story. There are several villages located within the jungle and two of them are named Changa and Manga. Now the question is that if indeed these two were fugitives, how could they have possibly established villages? I rather believe that when a railway station was built here, the villages of Changa Manga became popular and earned the forest its name. The reason why this jungle became famous with the stories of dacoits is that during the war of independence of 1857, which the British refer to as mutiny, several guerrilla fighters hid here. A few of the famous ones include Nazam Lohar, Malangi and Har Naam Singh. These are freedom fighters, as far as we are concerned, but dacoits to the British.'

Up ahead on the road, I saw two tractors laden with sugarcane blocking the way. When I approached closer they signalled with their headlights to slow down. As the car came to a halt just in front of them, Iqbal Qaiser broke his silence in a moment of panic and urged me not to stop. It turned out that one of the tractors in its miscalculation was trying to overtake the other, crawling around it. These weren't dacoits as he had suspected but inconsiderate drivers.

The historic city of Chunian, once a major army station of the Mughal Empire was sleeping. Passing through the deserted lanes and sleepy service stations we took a right. Chunian, like other historic cities, has scattered outside of the walls that once protected it from invaders. Driving on the outer road of this walled city, Iqbal Qaiser, who was relaxed now, pointed to a mosque in an empty ground facing the protective wall and said, 'Do you know that the story of Chunian begins from this mosque?'

In the darkness of the night we could only notice its silhouette. Stray dogs chased each other in the open field.

'There is a small structure inside the complex which was the *baithak* [place to sit] of Peer Jahania. After his death he was buried here. He was a Muslim saint during the Mughal era, and had come and settled at this particular spot. At that time this city was primarily occupied by Hindu untouchables. Defying the societal norms he gave a lot of love to the untouchables and eventually they converted to Islam. According to the *Encyclopedia of Sikh Literature* [p. 475], Chunian is the plural for Chuni which means pearl. I think pearl is used as a symbol to refer to those untouchables. Also notice how similar the words Chunian and Choda sound. Choda is a Punjabi word used for untouchables.'

There is something truly magical about this land. The shrine that we were heading to in the outskirts of Chunian belonged to a Muslim saint by the name of Baba Mast. I became particularly interested in the festival here after I learned that thousands of eunuchs from all over the country descended upon this shrine every year to honour the saint, the only one who gave them respect and love. Now the eunuchs return to pay tribute to Baba Mast. An overwhelming majority of the eunuchs have never seen the saint but have heard stories from their elders and are attracted to his shrine. The story of Baba Mast bears uncanny similarities to Peer Jahania, with both of them extending their love to social outcasts.

The eunuchs of South Asia, also referred to as *khusras, hijras, khwaja sarais*, etc., depending on the local dialect, inspire an evasive mystique about their character. Spotted in every major city, town and village of Pakistan their presence invites catcalls, offensive remarks, derision and profanity, yet at the same time their curse or prayer is believed to possess special powers. The treatment meted out to them is a strange hybrid of mockery and respect. William Dalrymple in his book, *City of Djinns*, aptly captures the essence of the phenomenon, 'The curious position of the eunuchs in Indian society can be explained by the head-on collision of two very different traditions, one Muslim, one Hindu...to give birth to a hermaphrodite is still considered by simple Indians to be one of the most terrible curses that can befall a woman. At the same time a *hijra* is considered to be unusually potent.'[32]

Historically, the eunuchs served as guardians of the royal harem in Mughal India. Their neutral sexuality made them ideal candidates to occupy the dual worlds of masculine courts and feminine harems. However, following the rupture of Indian society in the face of an onslaught from British colonials, like other repositories of tradition, they too found themselves misplaced in a culture that was aggressively breaking off ties from the past and bracing itself for modernity—one that was and still is defined as the Europeanization of society. Casted out of the royal harems, they were left out on the streets where they picked up songs and bawdy dances to eke out a living. They are also known to extend sexual pleasures to customers for petty sums of money to augment their income. In a Pakistani society torn between the interpretations of traditionalism and modernity, the presence of eunuchs on the occasion of weddings and childbirth is regarded as auspicious, and if their wishes are not fulfilled then the future of the wedding or the fate of the child are believed to be in jeopardy.

Jürgen Wasim, in *Journey to God*, alludes to the fact that in the South Asian tradition, Shivaism, a cult established around the worship of Shiva, explains partially the esotericism associated with eunuchs.[33] Shiva is known as Ardhanarisvara that is half male and half female,[34] with the right side being male and the left side being female. The two cannot survive without each other, and are reconciled by Shiva. This duality is also reflected in Shiva being seen as the creator and the destroyer.[35] The image of Shiva which is the union of linga and yoni is the ultimate symbol of the union of masculinity with femininity.

The sexuality exuded by eunuchs is a complicated combination of femininity and masculinity. At one level their makeup, appearance and an orchestrated 'feminine' body language help in the ideal representation of feminine gentleness. Standing on road junctions, they subtly flirt with young male drivers, softly caressing their arms, running fingers through their hair, trying to get some sort of monetary reward from them. On the other hand, when provoked they can be almost ferocious, shouting curses and gesticulating viciously. A eunuch's personality transforms easily from a genteel person to an uncouth man shouting in a husky voice. This dualism is the reason why eunuchs are regarded as potent and feared.

Provocatively dressed in skin-tight shalwar kameezes with low necklines, their tiny breasts thrust upwards, held by tight brassieres, which are always exposed, eunuchs dance passionately to vulgar Punjabi songs at Sufi festivals like the one we were heading towards. No festival is complete without their hip thrusting and breast shaking, paraded as dance. Jürgen Wasim makes an interesting comparison between 'this passionate dance at Sufi festivals and the *tandava*—the violent dance of Shiva, driven by an explosive energy which carries everything with it, as a mad explosion which accelerates devastation'.[36] Even though he makes this comparison with regard to a male dervish as opposed to a eunuch, the religious nature of the dance performed by the latter can be interpreted in a similar manner. He writes:

'The form and significance of the dervish dance may also be influenced in Indo-Pakistan by Shaivaism. One need only recall the position of Shiva as *nataraja* (Lord of the Dance) and the numerous interfaces between Muslim ascetics and Shaivite ascetics in terms of external attributes and behavioral patterns.'[37]

Shiva also happens to be the master of *lasya*, a gentle

lyrical dance full of sweetness and the reflection of all feelings of tenderness and love[38] along with *tandava* personifying the duality that only Shiva can encapsulate.

In contemporary Pakistani society, eunuchs occupy the lowest rung of social, political and, usually, economic order. Because of the profane activities that they engage in, intermingling with them on any social platform is frowned upon. One can interact with them at festivals or social occasions, even hire them for sexual pleasures but any sort of relationship outside of these contours is not acceptable. It is for this particular reason that when a Muslim saint, like Baba Mast, a respected member of the community, extended a hand of love to them, it became immortalized in the form of a religious ritual at this particular shrine. For the Sufi, on the other hand, the act becomes one of rebellion against the normative society and also a way of obliterating the social hierarchies defined by castes and classes. More importantly, the act serves the symbolic purpose of the Sufi debasing himself, an act of complete humility and negation of the self, to be submerged in the love of God.

Bulleh Shah, one of the most celebrated Sufis from Punjab, worked as the servant of a dancing girl for twelve years,[39] an act clearly meant to criticize the divisions of caste in society. Bulleh Shah was a Syed, and the dancing girls, like the eunuchs, occupy the lowest rungs of society. Musa Sahi Suhag, a fifteenth-century Muslim mystic from Ahmedabad, withdrew into the community of eunuchs to conceal his spiritual abilities.[40]

'We are almost there,' replied Iqbal Qaiser talking over the phone, as we neared the shrine. Before leaving Lahore he had called one of his friends who was a devotee and a regular visitor to the shrine and had been instructed 'to bring the car straight in'.

We drove through a sea of pilgrims on the crowded streets of this temporary village, surrounded by stalls on all sides. I ignored the volunteers working at makeshift parking lots.

We parked next to a jeep that belonged to Iqbal Qaiser's friends and entered a small tent, its ground covered by jute. There were about twenty people in this crowded space visiting the occupant—Mushtaq Hussain, a gentle-looking man with a thin white beard, wearing a faded white shalwar kameez. He is the spiritual descendant of Baba Mast and the current living saint. Behind him were a couple of houses built out of brick, large enough to incorporate several families.

'That must be his house, and this tent, his residence for the ten days during the festival. A smart political statement.' I scribbled in my diary.

'Please take our guests for langar,' Mushtaq Hussain instructed Majeed, Iqbal Qaiser's friend.

We were escorted to a room in the building next to the tent and served chicken alu as opposed to lentils reserved for the populace. My suspicions of making a political statement in adopting a simple life in a tent during the festival were strengthened.

'Please try this *chatna* with the food,' offered one of the men in the room.

'What is *chatna*?' I asked him intrigued at the blackish paste that was being presented to me. It looked like chutney popularly consumed with food in South Asia.

'*Chatna* is the masculine version of chutney.'

In this shrine of eunuchs, even the sexuality of food needed identification.

'This festival is the *urs* celebration of Syed Akbar Ali Shah who was the father of Baba Mast,' Majeed told us.

In the Sufi tradition, death anniversaries not birthdays, are celebrated with much pomp and fair and are known as *urs* celebrations. This is because it is believed that on this day the Sufi, regarded as the lover in mystic symbolism, unites with his beloved that is God. The union between the lover and the beloved is celebrated as a wedding. On studying Sufi literature and poetry, one would find references of the Sufi referring to himself as a female, eluding towards God as his beloved.

In the Sufi tradition, the male mystic taking on the persona of a female lover symbolizes the dualism of masculinity and femininity within one body, a metaphysical act of which the eunuchs are the living embodiment. Jürgen Wasim explains this phenomenon in the following way:

[*Malangs*] frequently appear in fantastic costumes, sometimes in women's dress; most of them wear jewelry....The females' attributes in terms of clothing, hair-do and jewelry make the feminine role clear which the *Malang* adopts with his way of life... Influenced by the popular mystic poetry of the Indus valley and the Hindu ideal of the *virahini* (the wife yearning for her husband), the *Malang* assumes the role of the bride... God is invoked as a husband by the devotee...this relationship can be understood as a sexual union, through which the man appropriates the deity in his innermost being. Sakhi-bhavaka, a subgroup of the Sahajiyya-Bauls in Bengal, to which Muslim sects also belong, men—dressed as women—identify with Radha, Krishna's lover...The *Malangs* desire to 'approximate' the female sex in order to fulfill their role as a 'bride of God'... Androgyny plays an important role in mystic tradition in the sense of a union of masculine and feminine powers. These ideas apparently go back to Shaivite influence.[41]

'Syed Akbar Ali Shah had four sons of which Khwaja Abdul Aziz Mast, also known as Baba Mast, was the eldest and designated as his spiritual descendant by the saint during his lifetime. He was particularly fond of eunuchs. Unfortunately I never got the opportunity to see Baba Mast myself but Mushtaq Hussain has, and he narrates several stories to us about him. Baba Mast used to say, "After my death I would ask God why He created the eunuchs the way He did. What is their fault? Why doesn't anyone love them?" Every year on the celebration of his father's *urs* he invited eunuchs and encouraged them to dance and play music here. One of his brothers, Ghulam Mustafa Shah, however, abhorred the practice. He was a religious puritanical, a fundamentalist,' Majeed said.

'In fact he was so strict about religious propriety that if two utensils touched each other while he was in the house he would refuse to have food saying that music has been created. Once while Baba Mast was away he asked all the eunuchs to leave as he thought their presence defiled the sanctity of the shrine. When Baba Mast returned, he along with all the eunuchs who had gathered for the *urs* festival, settled at the canal a few kilometres away from here. You must have crossed it on the way. With them also went the festivities of the festival. That year people abandoned the shrine and celebrated the *urs* at the canal. Ghulam Mustafa was left with no other option but to ask Baba Mast to come back and with him came back the eunuchs, music and dance, and they have remained here ever since,' he said.

I learned from the people attending the festival, that ever since this incident the canal had become the unofficial boundary of the saint's jurisdiction. It is believed that anyone who crosses the canal comes under the protection of the saint and can no longer be harmed. One of the eunuchs I spoke to told me that a person here once stole a bicycle during the festival but as soon as he crossed the canal he turned blind. When he returned his eyesight was restored. Every time he crossed the canal he lost his eyesight, and thus, he now lives here permanently.

'So is Mushtaq Hussain, Baba Mast's son?' I asked.

'No! He is the son of Khwaja Abdul Hayee who was a contemporary of Baba Mast and his senior at Dar-ul-Ulum.'

'What is that?'

'Dar-ul-Ulum is a madrassah in Deoband, India.'

'The founder of the Deobandi school of thought?'

'Yes.'

'But I thought the Deobandi school of thought was puritanical in its approach towards religion. Isn't it against shrine culture?'

'Yes. The Deoband school of thought today has taken a fundamentalist turn. However, it wasn't like that when it started. It became puritanical after Ashraf Ali Thanvi, the one who first translated the Quran into Urdu.'

Dr Tahir Kamran, a leading Pakistani historian, explains the rise of the Deobandi school of thought in his research paper 'The evolution of Deobandi school of thought in the Punjab' published in the research journal *The Historian*. He observes how throughout northern India, religious scholars called ulema were closely linked to political powers during the Mughal era. However, with the advent of the British their social status linked with the waning empire also declined. From this environment, a movement of puritanical Islam that aimed to remove all 'non-Islamic' practices from the religion of the Muslims took birth in the eighteenth century, spearheaded by Shah Walliullah. In contrast to them, the pirs or saints, the heads of large shrine establishments, syncretistic in their approach, supported the British government and in reward were dealt with generously.[42]

The Dar-ul-Ulum, from where the Deoband school of thought emerged, was established in 1867 by a religious scholar, Hafiz Syed Abid Hussain at Deoband in the United Provinces of India. This was a modern madrassah, different from the traditional ones in the way that it was organized and its curriculum designed. Organizational techniques from British institutions were adapted to serve the need of this Deoband school. It had a defined curriculum set by professionals and was affiliated with colleges that held regular exams. The school promoted a literalist reading of the Quran and Sunnah, urging its followers to focus on scriptural Islam as opposed to popular Islam epitomized by the saint and the shrine. This orthodox Sunni Islam 'imposes a uniformity of belief and practice through the extensive network of traditional schools and colleges'.[43] The school of thought gained popularity in the lower and middle echelons of the urban Punjabi Muslim populace, a feature that they have retained in contemporary Pakistan.

Post-Partition, the network of madrassahs affiliated with the Deoband grew exponentially, shaping the religious landscape of the country, transforming it from inclusive to exclusive. The rise of the puritanical school of thought has also fuelled sectarianism, an endemic that continues to threaten the social fabric of Pakistan. Dr Tahir Kamran notes several reasons for the growth of Deoband in the country, looking at the role of the monarchy in Saudi Arabia, the Iranian revolution and the Afghan jihad during the eighties.

In recent years, the focus of the Deoband has been on South Punjab and Sindh where there is an ubiquitous saint and shrine culture. Dr Tahir Kamran further observes that in the absence of a Marxist or a liberal ideology, the people of the South are attracted towards the Deoband school of thought, and feel victimized by the feudal nature of society intertwined with the saint and the shrine culture. Towards the end, he concludes that with the dominance of the Deoband school of thought in the country, there should be an increase in Islamic fundamentalism.

Sitting in the room noting down the conversation with Majeed, I heard a familiar Punjabi folk song being sung in a hoarse voice outside.

'Do you know the name of that song? It sounds familiar but I just can't place it,' I said, looking at Majeed, even though my question was directed towards anyone who was willing to answer. No one knew the name.

'We, Muslims, need to wake up and do something now. The extremists have hijacked our religion. The shrines follow the teachings of the Prophet [PBUH] and his companions. There was no movement in favour of Mumtaz Qadri[44] from any Sufi shrine around the country. As opposed to this you can see the role of the maulvis. The one at the Badshahi mosque refused to offer the *namaz-e-jannazah* for Salman Taseer and the maulvi who did eventually, had to go into hiding. It has recently come to my notice that the latest edition of the Oxford English dictionary also has 'Islamic extremism' as an entry. There is no such entry for Christian extremism or Hindu extremism. I don't think we can blame the British for that. It is because of the actions of the extremists,' Majeed said.

'Tell me more about Baba Mast,' I asked him trying to steer the conversation back to the festival and the shrine.

'After graduating from Dar-ul-Ulum he joined Sir Syed Ahmed Khan's Aligarh University and completed his studies from there.'

The educational background of the saint surprised me. Having heard about the shrine and the gathering of the eunuchs here, I had assumed that the shrine would be constructed around an obscure Sufi saint who would have stories of miracles associated with him, similar to Baba Aban Shah or the shrines of the sacred trees with doubtable historicity. However, Baba Mast was real and not only that, he was also trained in a mainstream religious seminary followed by a prominent university. His metamorphosis therefore into an eccentric Muslim saint and the founding of an exotic religious cult sounded even more intriguing.

'Baba Mast died without any progeny on 5 January 1995. He had nephews from his brothers but appointed Sahibzada Mushtaq Hussain as his spiritual descendant, transferring his spiritual prowess to him,' said Majeed.

'So what happened to the nephews?' I asked.

'They are still here. They look after the shrine and the festival. Mushtaq Hussain only comes during the festival and stays in the tent you visited. The nephews live in these houses around the shrine.'

'Doesn't that cause friction between them and Mushtaq Hussain?'

'It would cause friction if Mushtaq Hussain claimed anything. He comes here as a regular devotee. He does not practise *dum*[45] here nor does he take any share in the collections from the festival. All of that goes to the nephews. However, still there is one nephew who feels threatened by his presence and has tried causing problems for us a couple of times. He is the son of Ghulam Mustafa, the puritanical brother.'

'Will you celebrate Eid here as well?' I asked Majeed—the festival of Eid-ul-Azha would fall in a couple of days, while the ten-day celebrations of *urs* were being celebrated.

'Yes. I do not leave the shrine for ten days even if there is an emergency. I do this every year.'

One of the most celebrated travel writers of all times, Robert Byron writes in his book, *The Road to Oxiana*, 'While in India Islam appears, like everything else, uniquely and exclusively Indian. In a sense it is so; for neither man nor institution can meet that overpowering environment without a change of identity.'[46]

About eighty years after Byron wrote these lines, they continue to capture the essence of Islamic religiosity in South Asia, as the devotees of Muslim saints celebrate their festivals according to the local calendars as opposed to the Islamic calendar. The festival here is organized between the dates of 5 and 13 Kante, which usually fall in the month of the October in the Georgian calendar. The Islamic calendar, on the other hand, is calculated through lunar astronomy and therefore, its dates change from year to year and move across the Georgian calendar.

Leaving the room we headed towards the sound of the folk song. A eunuch was singing while male musicians played around him. Men from neighbouring villages, who had come to attend the festival, surrounded the performers. A couple of other *khusras* danced passionately, spreading both their arms outwards and pretending to fly. With their kohled eyes, they made intense eye contact with young patrons, inducing them to pay for the visual treat. Our guardians pushed around a few people to make way for us, forming a human chain around the girls to protect them in the all-male gathering.

The voice of the eunuch was coarse and off-key but the song was powerful enough to capture attention. He was about forty, heavily made up and wearing a pink shalwar kameez. Holding the mike with one hand, he held a lit cigarette in the other along with ten-rupee notes. The sound system was rudimentary, but it enabled the eunuch's voice to be heard in all directions.

In another smaller circle similar to this one, a couple of eunuchs with hair dyed blonde and mismatched makeup, danced to the songs blasting out of a cassette player, thrusting their bodies with vigour. Around this empty space, several small tents similar to Mushtaq Hussain's, were being used by groups of eunuchs who combed their hair and fixed their shirts in plain sight.

Next to a gathering of singing and dancing *khusras,* a group of about thirty to forty men and eunuchs sat supported by their feet around a cauldron, sipping a hot drink that was being served to them in communal cups.

'That is *kawa,* a speciality of this shrine. Baba Mast used to love having this tea and would prepare it himself for anyone visiting him. Would you like to have some?' Majeed asked.

It was strong black tea, heavily sweetened but without any milk. It provided an instant kick and I was wide awake once again. I made a mental note to myself to have another cup before leaving.

'This along with *chatna* is our speciality.'

We eventually found our way to the shrines of Baba Mast and that of his father. Taking off our shoes we walked on the small brick platform that led to a smaller enclosure containing the graves of the saints. Standing right in front of the shrines, three eunuchs wearing *ghungroos* (ankle bells) banged their feet on the ground to the beat of a song. The most ecstatic of them swirled around, his long hair flying around him—the *tandava* dance of Shiva.

The marble graves were decorated with frills and had epitaphs. A few devotees kissed the part of the grave where the feet of the occupant would be, while others walked around it. For the orthodox Sunnis, bowing in front of a grave is a supreme act of blasphemy. They believe that one is permitted to prostrate in front of nobody but God, and in doing so one is committing *shirk*. However, for the devotees of this shrine, this humble act of submission before the saint is not raising him to the level of God but only an expression of one's devotion. Whatever may be the symbolism behind this act, the very performance of it causes controversy between different sects and schools of thought.

'Would you like to have some?' Majeed asked, nudging me on the shoulder when he saw me observing a group of devotees sitting around a fire preparing bhang.

Other devotees sitting nearby were smoking hashish or cannabis. Their long matted locks fell below their shoulders on their colourful *cholas* (garments), fitted with patches of cloth of different colours.

This act of consuming drugs sitting around a fire in shrines is frowned upon by the general public and presented as an example of social problems that are promoted by shrine culture. While drugs are illegal in the country, the authorities allow their use at Sufi shrines because of their link to metaphysical experiences. However, as society has changed because of globalization of values and spread of puritanical Islam, the act of getting high at shrines is increasingly being seen as recreational instead of a religious tradition. Recently the Punjab government banned the consumption of drugs at a famous Sufi shrine in Lahore to control the law and order situation there, but in doing so it permanently altered the culture of the shrine, developed over thousands of years.

Like Hindu ascetics, the *malangs*, sit around the fire consuming hashish or other intoxicants like bhang. Bhang is marijuana pulverized, mixed with black pepper or almonds

and some sugar, dissolved in water and drunk.[47] In their poetry
and literature, the *malangs* have expressed their fondness for
hashish referring to it in several ways, a few of the famous
titles being: *al-luqaymah* (little green bite), *musilat al-qalb* (what
binds with the heart) and *waraq-i kheyal* (leaf of insight).[48]
Similar to other features of this version of popular Islam, also
known as folk Islam, anthropologists feel that these practices
are also derived from Hindu Shaivism. Jürgen Wasim points
out that for Hindus consumption of hashish, which is linked
to the cult of Shiva, enjoys a 'quasi-religious veneration'. He
elaborates that in Vedic literature the use of cannabis is
mentioned as a 'bestower of joy' and 'liberator'.[49]

The *malangs*, in a practice that is derived from Hindu
ascetics, use the ash from the fire that they sit around and
regard as holy, for healing purposes. Their long locks also
'signify the sear of life-energy and magic-like powers, one
example of which is Shiva in his avatar as mahayogi with his
long braided hair piled on top of his head like a pyramid'.[50]
According to Hindu mythology, the holy river Ganges flowing
out of his hair signifies its magical qualities. This mythological
interpretation when applied to *malangs* is a philosophical
metamorphosis of this belief—of hair being a seat of life
energy and magical powers.

Intermingling with the eunuchs, the *malangs* sat around
the shrine in makeshift tents, preparing their own food,
*kawa* and *chatna*. In an open field next to the shrine, were
the actual festivities of the *urs*. Flooded by lights there were
several small enclosures here where young eunuchs dancing
to vulgar Punjabi songs, were surrounded by crowds of male
onlookers. These eunuch groups had come from towns and

cities across Pakistan.

'There are about 2,000 eunuchs here,' said Majeed.

Most of the parties were staying in a camp next to the dancing arenas which were decorated with promiscuous pictures of Pakistani actresses. Leading the way and protecting us from thousands of onlookers, Majeed took us inside one of the camps where we got to meet the forty-year-old Kashi, while his guru, or the manager stood next to us, eyeing us with suspicion as we engaged in a conversation.

'I have been coming here for the past eighteen years. I have performed all over the country, at almost all the Sufi festivals, but I never receive as much respect as I get here. Outside, people humiliate us, beat us up and force us to do things we don't want to do, but here we roam around as badmash,' said Kashi.

'You know the same pilgrims are rude to the eunuchs the minute they cross the canal,' added Majeed, eager to promote the sanctity of the shrine.

Kashi was unimpressed by his justification but refused to comment. As his scepticism dissolved, Kashi's guru, Yasir, relaxed and said, 'The *khusras* are infamous for immoral activities all over the country but here no such activities are allowed. We don't come here for business but pilgrimage.'

He was referring to sexual business and not the dance business. He was holding a thick bundle of notes that he had collected from the dances outside.

'Here we are known as *Babe ki chidiyaan* [the birds of the saint],' he added.

At the sight of several sturdy men dressed in traditional kurta dhoti and turban and holding long and thick colourful bamboos, Majeed explained, 'These are the guardians here. Anyone who misbehaves with the eunuchs has to face their wrath.'

They were certainly intimidating. I wondered if it was the fear of these bamboos or the miracle of the canal that kept youngsters here from misbehaving with the eunuchs.

At the next camp, I sat next to Saima on the charpoy while one of her companions sat opposite to us.

'Is Saima your real name?' I asked her.

'No. That's my stage name. All of us pick up filmy names that we like. My friend calls herself Soniya. Billu and Sheela are dancing outside,' she replied with a giggle. 'I am a female born inside a male's body. Everyone used to make fun of me while I was in school. I was a bright student but couldn't study because of all the bullying. Students would make fun of the way I walked, talked and even moved my hands.'

Like other eunuchs, Saima has an exaggerated feminine body language. I have always wondered if this is a conscious attempt on the part of the eunuchs to exert their feminine identity, an aggressive rebellion against the physical constraints of the body or just a manner of enticing clients.

Saima, however, claimed that it was her natural way of being.

'At my home my brother would beat me up and no one would protect me.'

Her eyes turned moist.

'He would beat me up so that I stopped being who I was, a *khusra*. I left home when I was fifteen and have not seen my family since. I miss my mother but I can't see her. I think my brother and father are happy that I left. Maybe that's what they really wanted.'

'I didn't want to do this, this vulgarity. I wanted to study and become a doctor or an engineer like regular people. None of us are here because we want to. We are not permitted in any other profession. It is as if the world wants us to be who we are and then curse us for it. Only recently did the Supreme Court order NADRA[51] to issue us national identity cards. Imagine. We weren't even citizens of Pakistan despite being born here. The maulvis don't say our *namaz-e-jinnazah* and don't permit us to be buried in a regular graveyard, which is why we are buried in the darkness of the night.'

Beena, Saima's colleague added to the conversation.

'You know I have heard she-males in Thailand now serve as air hostesses. There is also a separate college for them where they are taught skills for all sorts of jobs. All we can do here is dance or have sex,' Beena said.

Facing the camps of the eunuchs were camps for prostitutes. We entered the prostitutes' tent and made ourselves comfortable on the empty chairs available. Surprisingly, there seemed to be greater interest in the show of the eunuchs than the prostitutes. I understood why when a group of young girls wearing jeans and t-shirts appeared from behind the stage and danced in a lacklustre manner to Bollywood songs from the nineties, unlike the eunuchs with their passionate thrusts. William Dalrymple in his book, *White Mughals*, makes an interesting observation about prostitution at religious festivals in South Asia, 'For in that strange link between piety and prostitution that existed all over India at this period [early nineteenth century]—both among the *devadasis* of the great Hindu temples and the Muslim courtesans who used to pick up their clients in the great Sufi shrines.'[52]

Here too at the shrine of Baba Mast, in a tradition that spans over thousands of years and links back to the tradition of devadasis—hereditary female dancers of the Hindu temples—prostitutes and eunuchs sell sex justifying the act in a 'semi-divine' idiom. Contrary to what Yasir said, a few eunuchs who I interviewed here acknowledged that if they are approached by a client, they do sell sex.

The last thing that Majeed wanted to show us before we left was a large flock of ducks in a vacant ground near the houses of the nephews of Baba Mast. 'All of them are from a single pair of ducks, pets of the saint. Over the years they have multiplied. Every morning at the time of the prayer, all of them gather at the *baithak* of the saint. We have seen it with our own eyes. It is a miracle. People coming to the festival bring them food to get blessings from the saint. They are known as *Baba ki batakhein* [the ducks of the saint].'

The *baithak* was a small place in front of an intricate wooden door, next to which was a stall selling religious paraphernalia, including pictures of the saint and his nephew. In the picture he was depicted as a weak old man, with long untrimmed hair and a thick beard, wearing a white shalwar kurta. There were also pictures of the young nephews of the saint cashing in on the legacy of their uncle. Facing the *baithak* was the *baithak* of Mushtaq Hussain, who, following the tradition of his spiritual ancestor, received pilgrims in his tents and offered them *kawa* like the saint did. My scepticism about him making a political statement rather than a genuine act of humility was wrong.

It was past midnight when we bid goodbye to our

hosts and headed back to Lahore. Crossing over the canal, leaving behind the sanctuary and the protection of Baba Mast we entered the kilometre-long stretch of road that connected Chunian with Changa Manga. Out of nowhere mist descended from the sky to add to the mischievousness of this road. A full moon shone all over the plain. At both ends of the road one could see the horizon, covered by mist, beyond which was unfathomable darkness. One rarely finds such a lonely road in the heartland of Punjab, the most prosperous province of Pakistan.

On Multan Road, the car's headlights caught the swirls of dust which rose up in the air and gently crashed on the windscreen, breaking the silence.

≈

Unperturbed by my presence, the dogs continued to bathe in the sun in the middle of the street at the footsteps of the shrine. All four dogs wore wreaths around their necks. I am used to the sight of stray dogs roaming around the cities of Pakistan. They never bite and are easily frightened by humans. Often in the morning I come across little children harassing a poor dog with stones and sticks. Literally hiding its tail between its legs, it finds the first possible opening to escape its tormentors. Usually when one walks too close to stray dogs, they run away in fear. But here were these dogs, lying in the middle of the market, unmoved by the presence of humans around them. The dogs, it seemed, were aware of the fact that they weren't ordinary. They were considered sacred at this shrine of Peer Abbas, the master of dogs.

Carefully walking around them, conscious of their

carnivorous teeth and the potential threat they posed to us, Iqbal Qaiser and I climbed the stairs of this newly constructed shrine, in the midst of a burgeoning trading city, Pattoki on Multan Road, a few kilometres from Lahore. The shrine was bigger than I had expected. In the middle of a huge vacant courtyard was the grave of the saint, a simple structure made of bare bricks with the epitaph on the tombstone reading, 'Peer Abbas Kutiyanali Sarkar', or Peer Abbas the master of dogs.

'Their numbers have decreased considerably. I don't know what has happened. The last time I came here there were about twenty to thirty dogs in the courtyard, freely roaming around the shrine, even sitting next to the grave,' Iqbal Qaiser told me.

'How long ago was that?' I asked.

'About fifteen years ago.'

'So there is no concept of impurity associated with dogs here because as far as I know dogs are considered impure animals in Islam, and their presence at a place of worship is frowned upon.'

'There is no such issue here. In fact the entire shrine is based around the concept of sacred dogs. These are the saint's pets and considered holy. His devotees present offerings to the dogs to seek the blessings of the saint,' Iqbal Qaiser explained.

Growing up in a Muslim home, I was bombarded with information about what is acceptable and what is not in Islamic culture—e.g., dogs are impure and therefore, are unacceptable as pets. Even though I had cousins who had them as pets, I never got one because of this notion. In order to satisfy their religious sentiments, my cousins, who had dogs as pets, argued that they kept them as guards which made it 'acceptable in Islam'. They also took particular care to never allow the animal inside their household or kitchen, an act that is likely to defile the purity of the space. Every time they played with the dog they cleansed themselves ritualistically, preferring to perform the ablution. During the holy month of Ramazan the servant was expected to take care of the animal as they avoided all physical contact.

So I was astonished when Iqbal Qaiser first told me about this shrine where dogs were regarded as sacred and presented religious offerings. We were driving near the city of Pattoki for one of our research trips when he pointed to a tall minaret rising from the midst of small houses and told me the story of the shrine of sacred dogs. Initially I imagined it to be a small place on the periphery of the city, an obscure religious establishment. When I visited the place I found out that it was regarded as a mainstream religious sanctuary within the city, whose sanctity was accepted by the local population. There were posters on the city walls declaring the dates for *urs* celebration, a huge affair attended by thousands of people. It was clear that the shrine of the sacred dogs had been accommodated into the mainstream religious sentimentality of the people here.

Islamic tradition has strict instructions about the impurity of dogs. According to Hadith literature, which is a collection of sayings of the Prophet of Islam, dogs are not to be allowed inside the house and if one ever comes in contact with a dog's saliva religious ablution is required. However, some sources claim the Prophet had a dog he played with outside the house. As opposed to dogs, cats are regarded as pure and allowed inside homes.[53] The Maliki school of thought is one of the most prominent schools of thought in Islamic jurisprudence. It holds that touching a dog entails an impurity that is removed by a lesser ablution.[54] A few other sayings attributed to the Prophet of Islam state that angels do not enter a house where there are dogs. Muslim scholars interpreting the Hadith have further stated, 'Dogs profane a mosque or a prayer place by their presence, a defilement that can only be corrected by physically removing them and symbolically washing the place they touched by earth and clean water.'[55]

While most Islamic traditions talk about the impurity of dogs, there is at least one tradition that focuses on the loyalty of the animal. Muslim scholars refer to a dog by the name of Qitmir who kept company with a group of young believers. Escaping persecution from 'non-believers', the believers took up refuge in a cave where they miraculously slept for centuries. The commentators regard Qitmir as 'a protective and loyal canine who would be allowed to enter heaven'.[56] One Hadith says that a person who gives water to a thirsty dog would be allowed into paradise.[57]

We exited the shrine disappointed at not finding any dogs inside the main sanctuary. Sitting in the verandah smoking his hookah was forty-year-old Jaffar Qazmi, a school teacher at the government school in Pattoki and the next in line to become the *gadi nasheen* or the head of this shrine.

'Once while Peer Abbas was returning to Pattoki it started raining heavily. He protected himself with his shawl but saw that a bitch and her puppies were drenched in the rain. The saint felt bad for them and covered them with his shawl while he soaked in the rain. After the rain stopped, Peer Abbas left for his next destination and the bitch and her puppies followed him. They remained with the saint after that day and became his devotees. Peer Abbas loved them and would present food and drinks to his pets before he had it himself. These dogs here are the progeny of the original dog that followed the saint. Do you know the saint had given his animals names: Wakil [lawyer], Havaldar [constable], Judge, SP [superintendent of police]?' Jaffar Qazmi said.

Later when I was researching the concept of holy dogs, the logic behind these strange names became clear. They were a mockery of the symbols of authority. Peer Abbas did not belong to a conventional Muslim Sufi order but to the Malamti school of thought. Jürgen Wasim describes the Malamti order of Sufis in the following manner: '[They follow] "free" Sufi orders...influenced...[by] indigenous South Asian traditions... [Malamtis are] those "who try to conceal their spiritual achievements", usually [by] violating religious laws on purpose...and [by] indulging in reprehensible behavior in public...Salvation for Malamtis lies in receiving disdain and humiliation from their fellow men...Often, they seek proximity to others who are socially disgraced and stigmatized.'[58]

At another place in the book he notes that their 'lifestyles [are] in apparent defiance of the establishment'.[59]

Ironically Peer Abbas was tapping on the same bias against dogs that he defied by his actions of keeping their company.

This was his way of inviting disdain from society so that he could diminish his vanity, more important to him than the concepts of purity and impurity. He found spiritual purity living in the company of the impure.

Peer Abbas is neither the first such Sufi saint nor the last one to keep the company of dogs. A few days after my visit to the shrine, I was telling one of my uncles from Sargodha about our discovery when he told me about another fakir in Sargodha who roams around the city all day long surrounded by dogs, and refuses to talk to any human being. Like Peer Abbas, he offers his food to the dogs first. The wandering philosophers of a school of philosophy in the eastern part of the Mediterranean, called the Cynics, exhibited a similar affection for dogs. This school of thought arose in the fourth century BCE as a reaction to the gradual dissolution of the Greek *polis* (city-state) and existed for around 1,000 years up to Late Antiquity.[60] Jürgen Wasim observes, 'Cheerful and enraptured they sought to enjoy life, disdained wealth and conventional etiquette, rejected religious laws and, as street preachers, propagated freedom and independence. Their wisdom was humorously expressed in jokes, parodies and satires'.[61] The word cynics comes from the Greek word of *kynikos* which means dog-like.[62] This is perhaps due to the fact that the cynics ate together with dogs, lived like them on scraps and slept in places that they shared with the dogs. They growled and yelped against the bourgeois ideals and conventions.[63]

The 'holy fools' of Christianity from whom the later itinerant dervish of the Muslim tradition emerged[64] are believed to have been inspired by this particular school of thought. The holy fools are also compared with dogs because 'they roamed around everywhere like dogs'.[65]

This implies that the practice of holy men taking up the

company of dogs dates back thousands of years. From the cynics it was passed on to the holy fools of Christianity, and then to holy men like Peer Abbas. Behind their eccentric behaviour and unconventional choice of friends lay a criticism of the materialism of the world, not through words but by actions.

Further explaining this connection between dogs and itinerant holy men, Jürgen Wasim notes, 'In India, a feral dog is itself called a dervish since he goes from door to door, begging for food. Islamic names with the component of 'dog' [*kalb*] are generally identified as loyal slaves and servants of a saint'.[66] In Persian poetry, the motif of the mystic and poet, presenting himself before God as a despicable dog is often found. This allegory can also be found in the poetry of the Punjabi mystic and poet of the early eighteenth century, Bulleh Shah, when he says, 'Dogs are awake at night, dogs are superior to you [believers].'[67]

In addition to receiving inspiration from Christianity, Islam in India intermingled with indigenous religious beliefs to take up a unique form, which is alive and thriving in Islamic Pakistan.

Writing in *From the Holy Mountain*, William Dalrymple points out that Shiva in his terrifying form (*ugra*), 'is accompanied by a pack of dogs; in iconographic depictions as a mendicant ascetic'[68] no different from the way Peer Abbas would have looked with his own pack of dogs. In Tantrism, Shiva in the incarnation of Bhairava, is depicted either with the face of a dog or has a dog as his vehicle. In Bhairav temples all over India, devotees offer prayers to the statues of dogs or living dogs. Dogs wander inside and outside the temple of Kalbhairav in Varanasi, and are garlanded by worshippers. Others present them with food offerings as a form of worship.[69]

'The dogs at the shrine are treated with particular respect because of their association with the saint,' continued Jaffar Qazmi. 'They have become famous as the dogs of Peer Abbas and whenever devotees visit the shrine to seek the blessings of the saint, they bring along food offerings like sweets, milk and meat for the dogs. They know that these dogs are the saint's favourites, and in order to please him they have to please them. No one is rude to them. I'll tell you about an incident. Once there was a man passing by the shrine holding a rope that was tied to a hen walking behind him. I was watching the scene from this verandah. One of the dogs of the saint snatched the rope from him and took away the hen. The owner could only look on in disappointment. You know if anyone causes any harm to the dogs of the saint they invite his wrath. There was a person who shot one of the dogs while the saint was alive. Peer Abbas, in his anger, cursed the culprit telling him that he would have to face hell in this world. Soon after the culprit suffered from a terrible disease and died. On another occasion, a person once whipped one of the dogs with a stick, as a result of which the saint cursed him saying he would leave his country and would never see it again. Even today he is living some place abroad and is not being able to return.'

'What happens if someone harms the dogs by accident?' I asked.

'It is for this reason that we have wreaths around their necks to distinguish them from the stray dogs that also roam around the city. This is to avoid any such incident, even by accident.'

'So what do the dogs do all day?'

'They just lie next to the shrine or roam around the city. Right now you can only see four-five dogs but there are about thirty dogs of the saint, who return to the shrine at one point or the other. The numbers have gone down since we stopped allowing the dogs to go inside the shrine.'

'Why did you stop them?'

'There are a few devotees of the saint who objected to the practice. They said that the shrine is a pure place whose sanctity is defiled by the presence of impure animals like dogs.'

'But when the saint did not have any problem living and eating with these animals, what right do his devotees have to object to their presence at his shrine?'

'I agree with you. This is what the saint wanted. But these people are his devotees and we have to listen to them.'

I wasn't convinced by Jaffar Qazmi's explanation. After all, he and his family were caretakers of the shrine and they could perpetuate the practice. Why would they listen to a fringe group of devotees? It was on the way back when I was discussing the issue with Iqbal Qaiser that the situation became clearer. Like other shrines in the country, this one thrives off the donations from devotees. The devotees who objected to the presence of dogs inside the shrine must be a powerful group whose donations constitute a considerable percentage of the total amount of money received by the shrine. The caretakers were happy to abandon the cultural practice of the saint while cashing in on his legacy.

'But no matter where the dogs are, all of them return on

the occasion of the *urs*,' Jaffar said.

'They probably return for all the food that the pilgrims bring along,' I joked.

'No. Actually for that entire week the dogs do not eat at all. Even if you put meat in front of them they refuse. Ask Nawaz if you do not believe me. He is the one who takes care of the dogs and knows them the best out of all of us.'

Sitting across from Jaffar on a stool was Nawaz Dogar, a sober looking man in his forties, who maintained a polite silence while Jaffar talked, and only spoke when allowed to do so. Due to his family link with Peer Abbas, Jaffar enjoys a special status amongst the devotees of the saint, such as Nawaz Dogar.

'When I was still a child I fell seriously ill. My parents brought me to this shrine and the *gadi nasheen* here recommended that I should be left at the shrine for a little while. I stayed here for a week during which I looked after the dogs, fed them, etc. When I recuperated I returned to my native village with my parents. However, when I went back, I fell sick again. One night in my dream I saw Peer Abbas who told me that I have been appointed to serve his dogs. In the morning when I told my parents about the dream they already seemed to know. Peer Abbas had appeared in their dreams as well. Since then I have been living here, looking after the dogs,' Nawaz Dogar said.

'How long ago was that?' I asked him.

'About thirty years.'

'You've been living here for thirty years?'

'Yes.'

In the middle of Nawaz's story, a female devotee came

and bowed respectfully in front of Jaffar Qazmi. She handed Nawaz a plastic bag filled with meat and left for the shrine. Nawaz whistled to the couple of dogs that were lying on the road and scattered the meat on the ground for them to devour.

'Tell me more about Peer Abbas,' I said.

'He was born in 1914, in India. He was highly educated, a graduate from Allahabad University. At the time of Partition, he moved with his family to a village in Jhang. He soon realized that he wanted to spend his life as an itinerant so he left his family and started roaming around the country. It was only in the last ten years of his life that he came and settled at this spot where he was later buried. He only did that at the behest of his friend, another spiritual master, Baba Jan Muhammad Mast, with whom he spent some time at his village. In fact while he was living there a couple of his dogs died and are buried there.'

'There are actual graves for the dogs?' I asked bewildered. 'I thought dogs in the Muslim tradition were not buried?'

'That doesn't apply to the saint's dogs,' whispered Iqbal Qaiser in my ear.

I noted down the name of the village and its exact coordinates for a visit to this shrine of dogs.

'Peer Abbas never married, so has no children,' Jasim Qazmi said.

'Who is the *gadi nasheen* then?'

'His brother, my father. Do you want to see him? He is too old to come outside, so you will have to come with me.'

We entered a small room behind the courtyard where an old fragile man in his eighties was lying on the charpoy, wide awake, staring at the wooden ceiling. We tried engaging him in conversation but he was hard of hearing and we got nowhere with him.

'When did the saint die?' I asked Jasim Qazmi back in the verandah.

'On 6 September 1968. Do you know he predicted his own death a week before he died so that all his devotees could come and pay their final respects to him? He was only fifty-four at the time. For a long time there was no shrine here, just the grave. This shrine was recently constructed by the department of Auqaf.[70] Its minaret now is the tallest in the city,' Jasim Qazmi said with a glint of pride in his eye. It had to give up its unique religious practice to become the tallest minaret in the city, I thought to myself.

Back on Multan Road, as we headed back to Lahore, we could see the minaret of the shrine rising tall from the middle of the city. From this distance, who could guess that buried within the city was this incredible shrine of sacred dogs?

As Iqbal Qaiser and I drove back quietly, depressed at how the shrine's tradition was being eaten away by puritanical versions of Islam, I wondered how many such shrines of idiosyncratic personalities lay hidden in Pakistan's bosom. My understanding of Pakistani culture and religiosity began to change that day as I tried to fathom the scope of its cultural and religious variations. The myths of uniform Pakistani nationality and religiosity began to shatter. However, with that realization was also the realization that now that I was beginning to explore these cultural aspects of the country, a new tide of a uniform religion was rising, whose tremors were already being felt at shrines such as these. I wondered how many of these particular shrines and practices would be robbed of their cultural heritage in the name of 'true religion' or 'true culture' before I would even hear about them.

≈

Located above a small canal, this small *khoka* (a small shop selling cigarettes, paan and cold drinks) looked like an overgrown version of a tin cigarette case. We were standing at Ada Ghaziabad, in search of the graves of Peer Abbas's dogs. A couple of months prior to our visit, an Urdu rap song called 'Wadera ka beta' by an artist from Karachi, had gone viral on the social media websites. The song criticizes the feudal culture of Pakistan, which is entangled with the shrine culture. Towards the end of the song, there are a few hilarious lines that say, '*Saeen tu saeen, saeen ke kapre bhi saeen; saeen tu saeen, saeen ki ghadi bhi saeen*'.

*Saeen* is a title used to refer to a feudal lord or a spiritual leader from lower Punjab and Sindh, where the shrine culture thrives. The lines say that '*Saeen* is unequivocally *saeen* but even his clothes and watch are *saeen*'; in other words, because of their association with the *saeen*, these objects become sacred as well. These last lines from the song became particularly famous, encapsulating the hold of feudal religious mafia on the politics of Pakistan. Iqbal Qaiser had not heard the song but had heard jokes that were based around these lines, one of which was, '*Saeen tu saeen, saeen ka kuta bhi saeen*' that even the dog is sacred.

How true was this line in the context of this particular shrine we were trying to locate. As I asked for directions, Iqbal Qaiser said, '*Saeen tu saeen, saeen ka kuta bhi saeen.*'

'There are two shrines of Jan Muhammad Mast. One is

on the right and the other on the left, depends on which one you want to go to,' shouted back the vendor sitting inside the giant tin cigarette box.

Gauging by the confused expressions on our faces, the shopkeeper explained further, 'At one of the shrines, the saint is still alive.'

Heading down the small road with huge potholes running along the canal, I joked with Iqbal Qaiser trying to cheer him up, 'What do we have to do with the living saints? It's the dead that we are more interested in.'

However, he was still upset at how small shrines were sprouting all over the country.

'You know I prefer these shrines to the puritanical Islamic movements. At least they are non-militant and tolerant,' I said.

'That's changing now,' he answered back. 'With the way Pakistani society has been altered following the war on terror, even those sects that were earlier peaceful and tolerant are not so any longer. Look at Mumtaz Qadri, for example. Bulleh Shah was a Qadri. The Qadri sect has a history of peaceful co-existence with other religions but that changed when Mumtaz Qadri murdered Salman Taseer.'

Despite my romanticism with the shrine culture, its indigenous beliefs and continuation of a tradition from the pre-Islamic era, Iqbal Qaiser made me realize that I could not close my eyes to the exploitation in the name of the 'peers' and saints that is a frequent occurrence in Pakistani society. Often one comes across news of a young married girl raped by the 'peer' whom she was visiting to seek a child. Many a time these cases go unreported because of the stigma associated with being polluted by the act, but also of remaining barren forever. He convinced me that this 'exotic' shrine culture was not the antidote for Islamic militancy that is creeping into the orthodox and puritanical movements of Islam.

We parked outside the village of Chak 22 which is where we were told the shrine was. One of the roads led outside the village, while the other went deep into it. It was a bright, sunny afternoon and the streets and adjacent fields were deserted. Up ahead from the road, an old woman, carrying a sack of freshly cut grass on her head, walked towards us. Rolling his window down Iqbal Qaiser asked the woman, who must have been in her seventies, about the exact location of the shrine. Putting the sack on the ground, she first covered her face partially with her dupatta and then asked us to follow the road that led into the village until it protruded out of the village and took us to the graveyard.

'That's where the shrine is.'

At a little distance from the village, the graveyard was located on a huge mound, created by the currents of the river Beas that once flowed from here.

'Look at those lines on the mound. That proves that this *pahari* was created by the river and not by the remains of an ancient civilization,' explained Iqbal Qaiser.

The mud track we had been following after our exit from the village ended abruptly in front of a steep fall. There was a small mosque next to where we had parked our car. A man, unshaven and wearing a dirty shalwar kameez, a thick layer of dust resting on his head, crossed us and headed to the mosque.

'This is the shrine of Baba Jan,' he said.

The courtyard where the mosque and the shrine were located was divided into two sections, one for each. The shrine was a simple single-storey structure, with a green dome on top, and a shaded verandah surrounding it. Ancient *waan* trees grew from within the concrete floor of the courtyard providing shade to the graves of the devotees of the saint, who must have paid hefty amounts of money to the caretakers of the shrine to be buried here. *Saeen tu saeen, saeen ki zameen* (land) *bhi saeen.*

I was surprised that Iqbal Qaiser had agreed to accompany me. His only child, a son, was to be married in a week's time and throughout our journey he was busy on the phone with different aspects of the wedding preparations. Attending one such phone call, he walked out of the shrine, facing lush green fields that unfolded in front of him. In the meantime, I walked around the shrine observing the graves, trying to imagine which one belonged to the sacred dogs of Peer Abbas.

After about fifteen minutes, still waiting for Iqbal Qaiser's phone call to end, I sat in the verandah, facing the shrine. The only other person there was circling around the room where the grave was located with his eyes closed, reciting verses from the Quran.

Sitting here, looking at this man religiously encircling the grave as he chanted in Arabic, I was transported into another world. I travelled back to a place several centuries ago, located in the heart of Margalla hills, where the federal capital of Pakistan is. There, in the ruins of Taxila, is a site known as Dharmarajika, a stupa around which are the remains of a monastery and giant sculptures of Lord Buddha and

Bodhisattva, dating back to the third century BCE. This site is a UNESCO world heritage site and a major tourist attraction.

This stupa is believed to have been constructed by the great Mauryan emperor, Ashoka, around the vessel containing the cremated remains of Lord Buddha. A few years ago when I visited the site, I walked on the pathway encircling the stupa, partaking in a ceremony that used to take place at that spot thousands of years ago. Walking along with me were the Buddhist monks and the students from the neighbouring monastery, carrying in one hand the golden vessel emitting holy smoke, chanting enigmatically from Buddhist scriptures. Sitting here, hundreds of kilometres away from Taxila, the vision of the Buddhist monks walking around the stupa was clearer than even before.

'How similar are these two traditions, separated by centuries; one which took iconography to new heights and the other, strictly iconoclastic, believed to be a departure from everything pre-Islamic, the dark ages of ignorance—*zaman-i-jahillya*,' I wrote in my diary.

'What department are you from?' the man who had been circling the grave asked me.

He had settled down in one corner of the room. It turned out his name was Allah Dita and he belonged to a city called Gago, which he said was about 'twenty miles from here'. The ceiling of the dome was decorated in gaudy glass patterns, and festoons and frills hung on top of the grave of Baba Jan Muhammad, covered by a velvet green cloth.

'I have come to offer my greetings to the saint.'

Allah Dita told me. This was not the first time he had come here.

Walking out of the courtyard from a back door, he led us to a residential building, where he told us we would find the guardian of the shrine. We sat down on the charpoy next to the door, while Allah Dita told the woman who stayed behind the door to tell the Syed he had visitors. While we waited for the guardian I couldn't help but marvel at the lack of human civilization around us. The only sound was that of birds chirping and the whistling of the leaves in the sweet autumn breeze. From far away, a droning sound of a tubewell drawing water from the ground reached us. Occasionally, there was the tinkering of bells hung around the necks of cows and buffaloes dragging carts on the mud tracks around the graveyard. A young peasant would probably be riding on the cart, basking under the sun and talking to his beloved on a mobile phone. Time stood still. Fifteen minutes could mean anything from an hour to two hours. Here time is not measured in terms of movements of the hands of the clock, but the movement of the sun.

'But why are you here?' Allah Dita asked us again, not completely convinced by our earlier answer. Dressed in western clothes, writing in English and driving a car, we displayed all the symbols of authority in this rural setting—an authority, which to these peasants, only resides with government officials.

'What department are you from?' he asked.

A dark-skinned man wearing a couple of bangles on his wrist walked out of the house. Allah Dita held both his hands and kissed them, as he stood opposite us. Slightly disappointed that we weren't devotees but rather inquisitors, he confirmed that Peer Abbas did spend time at the shrine.

'He spent thirteen years here in *chila*,' the man, named Syed Bahadur Ali, told us.

A religious rite of passage, the *chila* marks the period when the Sufi renounces the world, choosing a secluded spot for meditation. This tradition derives its roots from the early Christian monks who would spend a large portion of their lives living in caves. In South Asian culture, when this practice of seclusion for religious purposes interacted with the ascetic practices of tantric and yogic priests, they took absurd dimensions. There are stories of people hanging themselves on a tree for several days at a stretch to acquire spiritual prowess. In Lahore, I met a man who claimed to have spent forty days inside a grave.

'Peer Abbas also stood for a little while [as part of his *chila*] at Midhiyan wali bhani, the village behind us,' Syed Bahadur Ali said.

It was the village from where the sound of the tubewell came from.

'He buried two of his dogs there.'

'Are the graves still present?' I asked.

'Yes.'

'How do we get there?'

Having discovered what we were looking for, we turned down his hospitality and left for the graves. However, before leaving, more out of courtesy than curiosity, we asked him a few questions about Baba Jan Muhammad.

'Can you help me out?' Allah Ditta asked us as he walked along with us towards our car. 'My children have thrown me out of the house in connivance with my brother. They want my property. I went to the police but you know how they treat a poor man. Ever since then I have been visiting the shrines of various Sufi saints in the hope that someone will intercede on my behalf. You are from the media, right? Can you please do something about my situation?'

Leaving a cloud of dust behind we drove till the point the mud track permitted and then stepped into the fields, heading towards the trees that Syed Bahadur Ali had pointed out. As we walked on a small path in the middle of a rice field, there was the rustling sound of the crops swaying in the breeze. The drone of the tubewell was now distinct. A fiery sermon destroyed the tranquil atmosphere of the village. I couldn't make out what was being said but assumed it to be something about the 'blasphemous American, the makers of that ignominious movie *Innocence of Muslims*'.

Under the dried out trees on a platform were two small graves, with a small niche in the back, containing disused lamps. The niche was blackened, so we assumed that the villagers were lighting lamps here in remembrance of the sacred dogs. I wanted to ask a woman working nearby if the villagers still visited the shrine, but Iqbal Qaiser was concerned someone may take offence at us talking to a woman, even if she was seventy years old. Spotting a shirtless man tending to the wound on his foot, we headed across the road. He reluctantly shook Iqbal Qaiser's hand, but glared at me when I put my hand forward.

'Just tell me what you want? Stop this greeting business!' he shouted.

'We want to know about those graves there in the field?' Iqbal Qaiser retorted, trying to maintain his composure.

'I don't know anything. Go to the mosque or to the Dogars

[a caste] and they'll tell you.'

As we walked away from him he continued shouting. 'I know who you are, pretending to be interested in this godforsaken shrine from a hundred years ago. You are thugs!'

Next, Iqbal Qaiser asked a man working with a woman on mud pottery about the graves of the dogs. To my relief the man responded with a disarming smile.

'You want to know about Mohsin and Qamar?'

'Are those the names of the dogs?' I asked.

'Yes. Every year we arrange a festival for them which people from all the neighbouring villages attend. It is held around the graves. There is dhol, kabadai, halwa, etc.'

'There is also a *majlis*,' jumped another boy who had stopped to listen to our conversation. A naked child, a boy, barely able to walk, clung to my leg while we talked. The discomfort on my face was visible, so the man we were interviewing, Niyamat, pulled him away.

'When is the festival?'

'In summer, at the end of Jhet [local month]. The land behind the graves belonged to Peer Abbas and he used to work on it himself. Earlier at the time of the festival people from far away regions used to come here, but now the numbers have reduced. It is still a large event though.'

'*Saeen tu saeen, saeen ka kutta bhi saeen,*' said Iqbal Qaiser, sitting back in the car.

'What was that man's problem? Why was he so rude to us?' I asked.

'Never mind him. He is a Christian untouchable. Must have had a hard day,' Iqbal Qaiser replied.

'How do you know that?'

'You can always tell by their facial features.'

Iqbal Qaiser tried explaining to me the science of identifying an untouchable but I drifted into a world of my own, trying to find a reason that would have explained his rude behaviour.

# 6

## Animistic Cults

I ASKED ANAM STANDING next to me if she by looking at the title of the book could identify its genre. It didn't make any sense to her as well. I then turned towards Maryam if she knew what the book was about. In vain. As a young boy behind the counter prepared our coffee, I took out the book to see what it was about. Its title in Urdu on the other side of the cover made much more sense. It was a religious book that dealt with the topic of divine beauty being the only form of enchanting beauty.

Iqbal Qaiser buried himself in a collection of books on another rack. I walked over to discover that nearly all the 200 books that were up for sale here were religious. Writers and intellectuals in Pakistan, myself included, often lament that there is a dearth of reading culture here. I have often been told that there are certain topics pertaining to religion one should avoid writing about because of the negative backlash they are likely to invite. I, on the other hand, argue that one can get away with writing anything in Pakistan as no one reads. However, publishers and writers involved in the business of religious books have a flourishing business. If ever one comes across books in the homes of the upper-middle class in the country, they will inevitably be religious books.

Underneath the books were CDs and DVDs with Islamic messages: exposition of the Quran, interpretation of the Sunnah, religious hymns, etc.

It was still early in the morning and we had stopped at the first service station on the motorway for a pre-breakfast feast. Coffee, tea, biscuits, chips, gum were stuffed in plastic bags as we prepared to head off to our destination—Kallar Kahar, and the shrine of the peacocks.

'We'll have breakfast at Kallar Kahar after visiting the shrine,' I suggested.

After a drive of about three hours from our point of origin in Lahore, we got off the Kallar Kahar intersection and crossed the natural lake around which a thriving tourist market was emerging, and headed towards the city. After driving along the winding mountainous road, we took a turn towards the shrine. It was flanked by a flourishing market. A young boy handed me a parking receipt while vendors screamed from within their compact compounds, urging us to buy their paraphernalia: plastic toys, indigenous pottery, makeup, etc. Perched on top of the adjacent mountain, a bigger one, was a bare-bricked shrine which stood in isolation. Hanging between the two mountain peaks was a cable which drew a cable cabin between the two shrines. This was extraction of monetary benefits from religious pilgrimage at its best.

A few steps in front of the shrine we were visiting sat a mute beggar who tried to woo us by humming what sounded like 'Allah'.

'Please cover your head,' said a man to Anam while squatting on the floor at the entrance of the main shrine which held the grave of the saint. Maryam and Iqbal Qaiser remained in the courtyard which had been recently refurbished with marble, photographing the panoramic view of the valley of Kallar Kahar, at the edge of the lake. Contrary to my expectations, there were quite a few tourists here, taking photographs of each other with their mobile phone cameras. They were not serious pilgrims, but temporary devotees lured by the scenic view. There weren't any peacocks anywhere. I had received mixed reports about the peacocks, with some people telling me they didn't come to the shrine due to the increase in tourists and others claiming the peacocks did appear but only at sunrise and sunset. One of my colleagues, a local, told me that they are present here all the time. Choosing the worst possibility out of the three, I had mentally prepared myself for the disappointment.

Maryam too had given up hope of finding anything interesting while travelling with me, citing the example of the phallic shrine we visited together at Chak PS 50. Despite her deep disappointment I was glad she had agreed to travel with me.

There were a few devotees inside reciting the *fateh* (the first or opening sura of the Quran) for the salvation of the soul of the saint. I also held my hands together, standing silently at the side of the grave for a few minutes.

'It was so obvious you were pretending to pray,' Anam told me later.

'It doesn't matter if I say my prayer or not. It's for the people,' I said.

The grave, covered in a green shawl containing verses of the Quran, was beautifully adorned with garlands and a turban, placed where the head of the saint would be. It was decorated like a groom, the ultimate union of the lover with his beloved after death. The dome and the walls were decorated with kitsch glass patterns that have recently begun to dominate the architectural feature of Sufi shrines across the country. The simple yet intertwining floral and geometrical patterns of the past that emerged from an Islamic culture imbued in the scientific study of mathematics are no longer in vogue, being replaced by bathroom marble tiles or such glass patterns in the name of restoration.

Outside in the verandah, a marble plaque recalled the history of the saint. 'Darbar Sakhi Aho Baho Mooranwali Sarkar' it read.

It was obvious that the inscription on the plaque was tinged with state nationalism, the life of the saint reinterpreted to reinforce the separateness of Muslims from Hindus and the oppression Muslims faced while living in a Hindu-majority area.

'He is a martyr,' declared the plaque, 'and martyrs never die. He laid down his life helping the Muslims of this region against the Hindu Marathas. And now even the birds from heaven come to the shrine to pay homage to the holy martyr.'

The birds from heaven were the peacocks from the surrounding hills, found in large numbers in this region.

The plaque did not give any dates, nor was a historical context provided. While I struggled to read the Urdu text on it, I noticed a man who looked like a pilgrim from his sombre expression and worn-out clothes, stop consciously when he saw me. I assumed that he was circling around the grave in religious devotion, *tawaf*, and somehow my presence had distracted him.

'How long have you been here?' I asked the middle-aged man sitting at the threshold of the shrine, who had earlier advised Anam to cover her head while I entered without doing so.

'It's been a couple of years. I am a resident of this town, so I have been coming here for quite some time now.'

'Why is the saint called Moron wali sarkar [master of the peacocks]?'

'The buried saint is the grandson of Ghaus Pak himself— Hazrat Abdul Qadir Gillani.[71] The saint came to Kallar Kahar from Baghdad Sharif and brought these peacocks with him.'

'So all the birds here are from the progeny of that original muster of peacocks that came from Baghdad about 900 years ago?'

'Yes.'

Authenticity through foreignness as opposed to indigenousness remains a pathological problem in Pakistan, carved out of India on the basis of Muslim separateness. By acknowledging the fact that the people who now inhabit this piece of land are indigenous as opposed to foreign settlers, they would also be acknowledging that their ancestors were Hindus before they became Muslims, threatening the two-nation theory as it stands. In the collective imagination of Pakistanis, the entire nation is that of migrants from Iran, Afghanistan, the Middle East, Turkey and the Central Asian states—the land of the Mughals. It is also for this reason that almost seventy years after the creation of the country, it is grappling with issues of identity, struggling to define what really constitutes its culture. Vaisakhi, Basant, Mehndi and other such festivals are celebrated with a sense of shame with practitioners secretly admitting that these are 'Hindu' festivals and therefore not ours.

A few years ago, when I was researching for my first book at the Gurdwara Janamasthan, Nankana Sahib, the birthplace of Guru Nanak—the founder of Sikhism—a group of newly appointed government officials came and sat with the head priest with whom I was having a discussion.

'We, Muslims, have always liked the Sikhs. They are closer to our religion. We can reconcile our differences and become friends. It's the Hindus that we can never be friends with,' he said in a patronizing manner, as if giving the priest permission to continue living at a place where he really did not belong.

'Do you know sir that 90 per cent, if not more, of Pakistanis today have Hindu origins,' I said.

Shivering in disbelief he uttered, 'No. That's not true.'

'What's your caste?' I asked him.

'Rajput Bhattis.'

What is Pakistani culture, and what are its Hindu influences is an ongoing debate in the country. However, here at the shrine of the peacocks, this insecurity of national identity scaled new heights when the local government official claimed that even the birds are not indigenous, as if that would somehow make them less important.

'The birds used to obey every message of the saint,' he said.

'Why aren't there any birds here now?'

'They come only at the time of *fajr* [sunrise] and *maghrib* [sunset] when there are minimum people around. They come in hundreds. Earlier they used to be here throughout the day. That changed after the construction of the motorway.'

I turned to look at the road. I could see poles rising from the middle of the trees at the service station stop of Kallar Kahar, heralding the arrival of 'civilization'.

'Now with the lake and motorway, Kallar Kahar has become a prominent tourist destination. Tourists also visit the shrine, attracted by its location. The problem is that they don't respect the peacocks the way we do. Getting excited they start chasing the birds who fly away. That is why the birds have stopped coming here,' the man said.

'How do the locals treat the birds?'

'For us they are sacred. For example, if a bird is standing on the road, a local will not pass until the bird crosses over. The tourists try to catch them. We never catch the birds. We know exactly where they lay their eggs. If we wanted, there would be a peacock in every household of Kallar Kahar, but we don't do that.'

'Do people also bring offerings for the peacocks?' I asked.

'Yes. The devotees know that the peacocks are birds of the saint, so they take good care of them. But even that is changing now. There used to be no water here earlier. So women would bring water in pots from the lake below and place it here to seek the blessings of the saint. When there was no electricity they would light lamps here as supplication. But ever since the shrine has come under the protection of the Auqaf Department, all these facilities have arrived. We have electricity. We have ten huge pumps that can pull up water to this shrine any time of the day.'

'So devotees don't light lamps or bring water in pots anymore?'

'No,' the man replied.

What is interesting about the concept of a sacred animal or even a sacred tree, despite the superstitious and 'unscientific' rationale behind it, is its contribution to the preservation of the ecosystem. A tree that is considered sacred would never be cut, or an animal that is regarded as holy would never be hunted. Thus, the preservation and conservation of nature takes on a religious dimension as opposed to an ethical duty. However, when this 'primitive' attitude is replaced by a 'modern' one based on development, science and rationale, the sacred tree and the sacred animal become dispensable. Karen Armstrong in her book, *The Case for God*, argues that during a large part of human civilization, religious myths and stories were understood symbolically. She says that like poetry and art, religions also need to be viewed with an artistic interpretation, not in black and white terms. This literal interpretation is a result of modernity. So perhaps when these religious practices involving sacred animals and trees emerged, they were meant to be understood symbolically, reflective of a deep commitment to nature. However, with the arrival of modernity, not only did their interpretation change, but the relationship between the people and nature also changed. This attitude towards sacred space can be discerned from a letter that the Red Indian Chief Seattle wrote to the president of America in 1855, replying to the president's request to purchase their land.

At one point he says, 'How can you buy it [land] from us? We will decide in our time. Every part of this earth is sacred to my people. Every shining pine needle, every sandy shore, every mist in the dark woods, every clearing, and every humming insect is holy in the memory and experience of my people.'[72]

In Hindu tradition, peacocks acquire a special status because of their association with the deities Krishna and Sarasvati. A peacock is depicted as Goddess Sarasvati's ride, while the peacock's feathers adorn the crown of Lord Krishna.[73] Even in the Buddhist tradition, peacocks command respect as it is believed that in his previous life Buddha was a golden peacock.[74] The tradition of sacred peacocks that developed around this Muslim shrine in Kallar Kahar, is likely to have drawn inspiration from ancient religions irrespective of what the plaque says.

'What exactly is your job here?' I asked the man.

'I am employed by the Auqaf Department. I make sure that no immoral activities take place here. If there is a group of boys who have come to bother girls I ask them to leave. I also make sure that nothing unIslamic takes place here such as 'prostrating or offering *tawaf* around the grave. It is our job to educate people that they should only ask from Allah and not from the saint. We have written that as well.'

At the entrance into the main chamber were inscribed a couple of lines in Urdu that forbade devotees from performing these acts. This came as a surprise to me.

Shrine culture has always been heterodox in nature, condoning such acts of devotion. Closely monitored social propriety loses its stringency in the context of a shrine. Here females and males can intermingle freely. Social outcastes consume bhang and hashish, and those looking for immediate solace bow in front of the grave. Whereas a lot of shrines still retain these practices, it is evident that under mounting pressure from the orthodoxy which receives state patronage, some shrines are willing to concede to these demands, abandoning their idiosyncratic practices.

Sometime ago I was watching a news channel in which the anchor, a self-proclaimed vigilante, entered the shrine of Abdullah Shah Ghazi in Karachi, the most famous shrine in the city, and secretly filmed people consuming hashish. He began harassing the caretaker of the shrine for allowing such a practice. What was disappointing for me was the apologetic response of the caretaker. Shrines as opposed to mosques have historically gained popularity because of an acceptability they provide to people of all hues. They don't hold the standards of uprightness that mosques hold. However, under pressure, in front of the camera, the caretaker failed to explain the cultural context of the shrine and promised to monitor the situation better in the future. By barring devotees from performing acts of devotion at the shrine of the peacocks, the government's department of Auqaf has conceded to the fact that orthodoxy is preferred over heterodoxy. The irony is that they are putting an end to a cultural practice they should be protecting.

'Good story?' Maryam asked me as we headed out of the shrine.

'Yes. Interesting photographs?'

'Sure,' she said sarcastically. 'I'll make them interesting. I'll photoshop a few peacocks into the pictures and tell everyone there were hundreds of them here.'

'It's interesting how similar the shops and stalls are outside shrines and temples,' said Anam.

'It's the commercialization of religion. I think this is

one of the major reasons behind religious fundamentalism. Through mass production of books and CDs you give birth to a uniform religion, obliterating all differences—a major ingredient of fundamentalism,' I said.

'I was doing a course in college for which we had studied the phenomenon of commercialization of religion. Earlier what was sacred was also elusive. Now it has become accessible. It changes the way we understand religion,' she replied.

Commercialization of religion allows it to be possessed by its buyer, a tangible product that could be shoved into the face of those who do not 'believe'. It strips the religious ethos of its striving, the pain of working towards becoming a better human being. Now, one can just pay to become one.

'This won't fall, will it?' asked Maryam sitting in the cable cabin.

'If it falls just pray that we die. I don't want to live in a coma or worse, be bedridden for the rest of my life,' replied Anam.

As the cabin shook in mid-air I asked the girls to stop catastrophizing. We were flying to the other shrine, across the mountain.

'There isn't anything there except for *rori* [rocks],' a scary-looking man had told us as he herded us into this encaged cabin. He had recently moved to Kallar Kahar from Dir, fleeing the insurgency there and looking to reap profits from the burgeoning religious tourism. Behind him swayed a Pakistani flag with a picture of Mickey Mouse on the white section (reserved for minorities) and Allama Iqbal and Jinnah on the green section. Commercialization of nationalism? Just as dangerous as that of religion.

'It's ironical how Mickey Mouse is on the Pakistani flag that represents our nationalism, which is defined by our anti-Americanism,' said Anam.

How embedded is the folk religion, epitomized by such small shrines, in the local geography I thought, trying to distract myself from the frightening realization of dying in the course of researching for this book. It shows the strong bond the people have with their surroundings, a sense of rootedness, which challenges the notion of nationalistic religion that wants us to believe that we are all migrants in our own land. The saint here becomes the saint of the rocks.

Reading the shrine's history inscribed on a plaque that hung on the wall of the shrine, it was obvious why this particular shrine was ignored by government authorities unlike the neighbouring one. This shrine's saint, 'Bawaji Muhammad Alim Fazl Shah Baghdadi' was not a warrior- like Saint Aho Baho. Accompanying Saint Aho Baho from Baghdad, he chose to spend his time quietly on top of this mountain in the remembrance of God instead of fighting. He didn't fit the nationalistic discourse and was therefore irrelevant.

Unperturbed by our raucous voices that disturbed the peace of the surroundings, an old man silently sat next to several pots of water. Water pumps have not reached here as yet so carrying water pots to the top is still a sacred duty.

'Where is Takht-e-Babri?' I asked Iqbal Qaiser as we walked around a meadow on top of the mountain.

'Right there,' he said pointing to a small minaret behind a house.

'Let's walk there,' he said and without waiting for me to reply started descending the trail.

'Can we go in the car instead? It's on the way anyway and we are already short on time,' I said.

'Sure,' he replied.

≈

In 1519, Babur crossed over river Indus, then the unofficial border of India, along with his army that had increased gradually since his departure from his kingdom Farghana, where he was robbed of his throne. In India he laid the foundation of what became the most powerful empire of its time—the Mughal Empire. In his memoir, *Baburnama*, he meticulously notes down his journey, also choosing to talk about the geography, fauna and flora, and people of the lands he had crossed. On 20 February 1519, on his way back from Bhera, a historic city on the bank of river Jhelum, he had camped at Kallar Kahar. This is what he had to say about Kallar Kahar:

'In the middle of it is a lake some six miles around, the in-gatherings of rain from all sides. On the north of this lake lies an excellent meadow; on the hill-skirt to the west of it there is a spring having its source in the heights overlooking the lake. The place being suitable I have made a garden there, called the Bagah-i-Safa...It is a very charming place with good air.'[75]

The garden no longer exists, having made way for several houses and orchards. A board on the main road reads 'Takht-e-Babri' or the throne of Babur and points towards the mountain. Hidden in its embrace is a small black structure carved out of rock that used to serve as the throne of the Mughal king. It is an unimpressive structure. This was to be the first Mughal landmark in India, an embarrassing prototype of the splendid architectural tradition that was to flourish.

A plaque raised here recently recalls the history of the monument. It states that this structure was constructed by the army of Babur in the middle of the garden, and standing here Babur had addressed his force. The plaque also mentions that wild peacocks roam around in this jungle and no one disturbs them.

Elevated to the top of the structure, I tried imagining hordes of Afghans and Turks and what Babur would have said. Would he have lured them with a description of the endless bounty that was to flow from the exchequers of India? Did he inspire them with religion? Whatever he had said, there is no doubt that this less-than-ordinary structure, a blemish on the Mughal architectural tradition, had immense historical importance as it marked the beginning of the Mughal Empire in India, a phenomenon that was to last for about three centuries.

≈

Stuck in the traffic jam of Bhera, a city towards which Babur had headed from Kallar Kahar, I could feel myself losing control and succumbing to road rage. The traffic in the cities of Pakistan is as intolerant as religious fundamentalism. And this is not just a humorous comparison but rather a symbiotic relationship that I believe could be studied further by sociologists. In the past decade, road rage and an utter lack of respect for other drivers on the road, have been growing. Iqbal Qaiser has an explanation for this growing intolerance.

'There used to be a Punjabi phrase, *"oh jane"*, which people would use when there were intellectual disagreements.

They would say "*oh jane*" to mean that we don't know what the truth is and God knows better. The phrase has become extinct now, as a result of which I believe that intolerance has increased. There is no more room for obscurity, of not being sure,' he told me.

A few years ago, Iqbal Qaiser and I had come to explore the city of Bhera. We walked around its narrow alleys, marvelled at its intricate woodwork, specimens of which are also present in the Lahore museum, and explored its abandoned temples with their cone-like towers piercing the sky. We came across a temple on the outskirts of the city, a single-room temple with a *shivling* at the centre around which were blackened lamps still containing oil. This meant that they had been used recently. Following us, a young boy entered the temple and told us that the locals still lit lamps at this abandoned *shivala*.

'One day a few women saw an old man wearing a white shalwar kameez and sporting long, white hair and beard inside the temple. When they followed him inside he disappeared. He was a sage. Ever since then the locals here have lit lamps at the temple.'

These are all Muslim families, Bhera having exiled all its Hindus in 1947.

Driving along the circular road that circumscribes the walled city of Bhera, I looked for traces of the temple but couldn't find any. A lot of new houses had been constructed on vacant plots. Maybe the temple was hidden behind some wall or incorporated into one of the houses, I thought to myself. Given the local myth about a sage who appeared in the temple, it was unlikely that the temple had been razed.

Superstitious villagers and small-city folk would be too scared to invite the wrath of the supernatural.

≈

'Could you please slow down?' asked Iqbal Qaiser as he peered out of the car window. 'There is a gurdwara here somewhere and I want to photograph it.'

We were still a few kilometres from Phalia, our next destination, after which we were to head to Gujrat, fifty kilometres away. I wanted to get there while there was still some light.

From Kallar Kahar, crossing Bhera and Mandi (market) Bahauddin, we were now in a small market town called Mandi Mangat. This town was once an obscure village and had flourished after a railway station was established here by the British during the late part of the nineteenth century. Now, however, the railway station has been abandoned as Pakistan Railway passes through its worst economic crisis ever. Slowly it seems, Mandi Mangat is receding to its original peripheral position.

Excitedly pointing towards an ancient stout structure in the middle of an empty ground, Iqbal Qaiser instructed me to stop the car. It was a splendid building, well-preserved and lying vacant in a vast ground. It was surrounded by protective walls on all four sides, and all the entrances to the gurdwara had been blocked to protect it from loiterers and drug addicts.

We sneaked in through a small hole that had emerged in the middle of a wall, followed by a group of local boys, who joined us out of sheer curiosity. A corrosive ash had settled over the white structure of the building, but its condition was much better than other such shrines I had seen. The building had frescoes depicting Hindu deities, women in harems and floral patterns. A few of the faces had been chipped off.

'This is done by the local boys,' said Amir, an eighteen-year-old boy who had decided to be our guide.

This was because of the belief that it is unIslamic to draw a human face. I thought about the young, impressionable children learning about what is acceptable in Islam and what is not, taking upon themselves the task of Islamizing their surroundings.

'Look at this,' said Iqbal Qaiser pointing to a figure of a woman smoking a hookah. 'This, in a gurdwara?' he questioned with a smile.

'Consumption of tobacco is forbidden in Sikhism,' I explained to Anam who was perplexed at Iqbal Qaiser's comment.

A graffiti on the gurudwara's wall urged visitors to respect the holy words written on the walls. This was a reference to several religious edicts that were engraved all over the building.

'Who is in charge of the gurdwara?' I asked our young guide.

'He was a landlord from the town. That's his house,' he said pointing to a large white construction a few metres away from us. 'He would take good care of this building. But now we don't know who is in charge. That man is dead. We don't know what will become of the gurdwara.'

'What is the history of this gurdwara?' I asked Iqbal Qaiser[76] once we were back in the car.

'This was the house of Bhai Bannu, who was a devotee of the fifth Sikh guru, Guru Arjan. The current structure was raised by Maharaja Ranjit Singh. It was a huge gurdwara with its boundary wall starting where the main road is. There was a pool next to it which has been filled and the land occupied by squatters. Every year, in that vacant ground in front of the building, there used to be a festival on the occasion of Vaisakhi.'

'The Sikhs still come,' I interrupted. 'Not really for the festival but on the occasion of Vaisakhi. When they come from India and other parts of the world to Hassan Abdal they also visit this shrine. Amir, the boy who was showing me around, told me.'

≈

My interest in the city of Phalia emerged when I found out that it was named after Alexander's legendary horse Bucephalus— Phalus became Phalia. I was told the horse had been buried here and his grave still existed.

Upon entering the city I called up Salman Rashid, who has written extensively about the trail of Alexander, to confirm what I had heard.

'The horse is not buried here,' he said to my disappointment. 'He was buried near Jalalpur on the other side of the river's bank where his grave was swept by the flood only a few months after. Coins dating back to the Indo-Greek era were discovered from the *pahari* of the city of Phalia, giving birth to the rumour that Alexander had come here and the horse was buried on this side of the river.'

'Is at least the name Phalia derived from Phallus?' I asked.

'No,' was the reply, crushing all my hopes of linking the history of this city with the legendary horse.

'This version became popular during the colonial era when British officers roamed all over the country collecting oral history. Some old fanatic Baba must have told the then deputy commissioner about this version and it became part of history.'

'We could at least visit the mound. Do you know where it is?'

'Just ask any old person from the city about the old mound. There is a government office there along with a school,' Salman Rashid replied.

We stopped next to a shop in which a man in his mid-seventies was sitting, and Iqbal Qaiser went inside to ask him about the exact location of the old mound.

'Congratulations,' Iqbal Qaiser said as he returned. 'That *pahari* has been sold by the department for nine crore rupees. Now there will be a shiny, new shopping plaza there.'

≈

Burying of horses or other animals is not a common tradition in South Asia. This honour is reserved for a few special animals, either associated with a conqueror as in the case of Alexander, or Qammar and Mohsin in the case of Peer Abbas's dogs. A few months prior to our visit to the shrine of the sacred peacocks, Iqbal Qaiser and I had visited a shrine of a sacred horse.

≈

Pointing to a tall pole that looked like a mobile tower, Iqbal Qaiser told me that's where we needed to go. An orange flag, symbol of the shrine, swayed in the early morning breeze. We were driving around the neatest and most expensive residential area of Lahore, the Defense Housing Authority (DHA).

We tried following the direction of the flag and ended up in front of a wall. Recently constructed, the DHA sprawls across a vast tract of land, eating into the small historic villages in the area. Congested and inflicted with poverty, these villages are now an anomaly within this grandiose housing society with its wide roads and uniform palm trees imported from the Middle East. In order to preserve the area's beauty, the villages have been trapped within a wall, a hole that they have dug for themselves by selling their abundant land for peanuts to the housing authority.

I manoeuvred the car through the mud track that passed off as a road, and reached the edge of the village called Amar Sadhu, while constantly keeping an eye on the orange flag. Conveniently ignoring a group of devotees sitting under a banyan tree, we headed towards the further end of the compound where Iqbal Qaiser wanted to show me the gurdwara around which this Muslim shrine had emerged.

'They might stop you from taking photographs, so it's better to get done with the photography and then talk,' he said.

Travelling and photographing for much longer than I have, Iqbal Qaiser has learned through bitter experience that not everyone is supportive of the idea of allowing their house or shrine to be photographed. He has been beaten up by police officials, held in detention for hours by the army and even accused of being an Indian agent.

The gurdwara was a splendid building—small yet sturdy. As we photographed the remains of the once beautiful structure, a lean man walked unsteadily behind us into the gurdwara.

Built in honour of the memory of the sixth Sikh guru, Guru Hargobind, this gurdwara is known as Gurdwara Bibi Kaulan.[77] Bibi Kaulan was a maid employed by a Muslim trader who lived in Mozang. The trader had bonded her against her wishes. One day when she heard that the guru was encamped nearby she came to him and pleaded for her rescue. The guru took her along with him on his horse and they reached this spot where they rested for a while before they headed off to Amritsar.

'The story of the gurdwara is also affiliated to the guru's horse like that of the Muslim saint's horse,' said Iqbal Qaiser.

'In Amritsar, the woman insisted that the guru give her his name, or in other words, she insisted that he marry her,' he added. 'The guru obviously couldn't marry her but the woman insisted. So in order to satisfy her, he ordered the construction of a pool in Amritsar near the Golden Temple and named it after her. Furthermore, he decreed that anyone visiting the Golden Temple to pay homage must first perform ablution at the pool of Bibi Kaulan.'

'Where are you from?' asked the lean man who was following us, but we continued to ignore him. The roof of the shrine had vanished, while the black and white tiles on the floor were in a dilapidated state. 'When will this appear in the newspaper? That used to be the pool of the shrine,' he added pointing to wild grass growing in an empty space. 'After Partition the gurdwara was abandoned so Baba Mastan Shah decided to come and live here. Now this has become his shrine.' His grave along with those of his progeny was in a single-storey room facing the gurdwara.

We sat down under the banyan tree with a group of dervishes.

'Baba Mastan came here sometime around the tenure of Ayub Khan on the order of his *murshad* [spiritual master],' said a senior dervish who wore only a loin cloth.

He sported a couple of necklaces made out of colourful beads and wore several rings on his fingers.

'His real name was Baba Riaz Shah but his devotees called him Baba Mastan.'

As the dervish recalled the history of the saint, I pretended to show interest, but my mind was preoccupied with the holy animal buried here.

'Mai Rani, you mean,' replied the dervish to my question about the mare. 'The saint was very attached to her. But unfortunately she died while Baba Mastan was still alive. He ordered that she should be buried and instructed all his devotees to pray at the grave of Mai Rani before coming to his grave. That's her grave,' he said pointing to a long grave in the middle of two rooms next to the entrance. 'The saint said that if any of your prayers are not answered at the grave of Mai Rani, then you should stop calling me Baba. On the occasion of the celebration of his *urs* we also celebrate the *urs* of the mare.'

Needless to say the dervish or his companions did not share my fascination for the story of the mare. For them it was an ordinary tale and a normal ritual. The conversation reverted quickly to the miracles of the saint and I dug myself deeper into my notebook searching for an escape.

'And you know the saint travelled a lot,' said the dervish, a comment that ignited a fire of curiosity in me.

Blocking out his other words I got lost in my imaginary world, contemplating the sociological interpretation of this mundane comment.

Travel has always been an integral part of a saint's life in this part of the world: Hindu, Muslim, Sikh alike. The Sufis gained prominence in a world devoid of today's connectedness, when even to travel from one city to another within a country was a daunting task because of hostile routes, bandits and animals. Their knowledge of different cultures, religious practices, food, etc., gave them access to a world that ordinary people were not aware of, elevating the status of the Sufi in a caste-ridden society.

'Baba Mastan would tell us stories from his travels,' said the dervish.

'Why don't you also cover the shrine of Ghore Shah for your book,' suggested Qaiser as we headed back.

'The shrine with the toy horse offerings?'

'Yes.'

≈

My photographer friend, Rida, photographed an elaborately designed tombstone with floral sculptures. Most of the graves were made of mud, with no mark or inscription identifying their occupants.

'What is this way of making graves? These aren't allowed in Islam. Graves should be simple like those there, made out of mud,' she commented putting her camera back in the cover.

For her this was a harmless observation, a critique of the elaborate tombs constructed over graves which became objects of veneration and centres of religious exploitation of a different sort, but I was taken aback. This remark that came from a liberal arts student, the last bastion of hope in the Pakistani educational system, for a secular and religiously tolerant society, was a shock. It reflected her religious perspective, her sectarianism. The religious puritanical Wahhabis of Saudi Arabia believe that graves should be simple, while many other sects predominant in Pakistan have a lenient view on the elaboration of graves. So death after all is not really the end. Religious nuances and sectarian differences continue to haunt individuals even when they are in their graves.

I took a short walk around this historical graveyard situated in Sultan Pura, the heart of Lahore. It was a Sunday morning so several families had gathered around the graves of their loved ones. In a vacant area, a few children played cricket. Walking carefully around the graves, I stumbled upon a junkie hidden in between two elaborate tombstones, collecting syringes in a discarded plastic bag that earlier carried flowers for a departed soul. Abandoned by their families and derided by society, junkies often end up finding a permanent abode in this land of the dead. It is interesting that this new group of 'devotees' to the shrines residing in graveyards is also a legacy of the Islamist dictator who in his puritanism expelled a former group of devotees from the shrine. The popularity of Wahhabi Islam in Pakistan under the guidance of General Zia-ul-Haq dates back to the Afghan jihad unleashed during the Soviet occupancy of Afghanistan in the eighties; and in retaliation the Afghanis sent back their cultivation of surplus poppy seeds—heroin.

Scattered all over the graveyard were broken pieces of small horses made of mud, painted in white with colourful stripes; these mud horses are offerings at this shrine of Ghore Shah, the master of horses. At the entrance was an old man whose family had migrated from Jalandhar during Partition. He claimed to be a descendant of a family of caretakers of this shrine and managed a small stall selling the toy offerings. Behind him was the enclosure with the grave of the saint at the centre of the courtyard, flanked by graves of his devotees and family members. His name at the base of the tombstone read 'Hazrat Syed Bahauldin Jholan Shah Bukhari Suhrawadi'; 'Date of death 1594'. Next to the tombstone were several toy horse offerings in a line. Outside the courtyard, within the complex of this ancient graveyard was a small mosque while across the road, the minaret of another mosque soared higher than any other building. I wondered which sect of Islam did that mosque belong to.

According to folk legend, there was a time when instead of these mud objects, real horses were presented at the shrine. The saint, who died at the age of five, loved riding horses, a love affair that continues till date.[78] His devotees believe that by offering horses, they please the child-saint who then fulfils their wishes. Suffering from palsy, the child-saint would shake uncontrollably earning him the title of Jhole Shah. Due to his love for horses he became known as Ghore Shah. He was also a child with special needs, hence a Wali, someone who could intercede with God on behalf of ordinary people. Jürgen Wasim notes, 'In West and South Asia, people treat the truly mentally disturbed with remarkable patience and indulgence since their symptoms are often understood as manifestations of the divine.'[79]

Elaborating further, he says that they are regarded as the

favourites of God because of their complete disassociation with the world, which imply ultimate resignation for the Divine.[80]

Like other folk stories that have developed around Sufi shrines and cults, the historical veracity of this folk story cannot be established due to a lack of written records. Those that are available belong to the nineteenth century, written almost 300 years later by British colonialists on the basis of the oral testimonies of the practitioners. What casts doubt over the authenticity of this story is the similarity between these toy horse offerings and those that have been unearthed from the Indus Valley Civilization, believed to have been used in religious cults like this one. The only difference appears to be the colourful stripes. This led me to conclude that like the other folk religious cults discussed earlier, this one also originated in the depths of antiquity. For the devotees here, ignorant of the ancient connection, the story of Ghore Shah aka Jhole Shah presented a neat reference point, a much needed rallying point for the ritual. Perhaps there was a child by this name who, on observing these religious offerings, was fascinated by them and had been buried here after his death.

'Who makes these horses?' I asked Allah Rakha, the vendor.

'The *deendars* make them at Chinatown.'

*Deendar* refers to Muslim converts who were originally Hindu untouchables; the title being a mechanism to maintain a system of caste hierarchy in Pakistan. A major school of thought in Indian archaeology believes that the untouchables of the Vedic society were the original inhabitants of the Indus Valley Civilization, reduced to that status by the conquering Aryans who had come on chariots and destroyed these cities, laying the foundation for a new civilization on the banks of the Ganga and Yamuna rivers. This process is believed to have started around 1500 BCE, the period which saw the decline of the Indus Valley cities. There are other prominent archaeologists, like Mary Kenoyer, who deny the Aryan invasion theory and argue that Aryans are indigenous people who occupied the cities of the Indus Valley Civilization. In the context of this shrine, an interesting point to note is that former untouchables are still engaged in a religious cult that might have its origins in the Indus Valley Civilization, and irrespective of whatever becomes of the Aryan invasion theory, there is no doubt that they are indigenous people of this land.

≈

We reached Gujrat at around three in the afternoon, so there was plenty of time to take photographs in the light of the sun.

Seeking directions for the shrine of the 'Master of crows' we came face-to-face with a huge poster of the saint, squatting on the ground with a long white beard and hair, and wearing nothing but a loin cloth. Around him were a few crows feeding off the food that he had scattered on the ground. 'Follow the posters,' suggested Iqbal Qaiser and I did, ending up right in front of the shrine.

There were several pilgrims here, women, men and children, to offer their respects to the saint, who seemed to have quite a following in this historic city. On a railing that bordered the walls covering the shrine on all sides, I saw a few crows sitting peacefully, while below them, a cat fed from the pots containing offerings for the crows. A pair of swans flew in to share the feast. A young girl walked to the corner reserved for the birds and placed some rice into the overflowing pots. There were many more crows flying from one peepal tree to another around the shrine. I was glad there were some sacred birds around, particularly for Maryam to whom I could boast later.

The room where the grave of the saint was placed brimmed with devotees offering their *fatehas* and reading the Quran. Behind it was an ancient *waan*, another sacred tree in the Indo-Pak context, under which several devotees had lit lamps.

'Is this a grave?' a young girl asked another girl playing with the lamps.

'No, stupid. This can't be a grave. If it was, why would there be a tree in the middle?' was the reply.

A police official began to follow us while we were photographing the shrine, after a young male employee of the Auqaf Department forbade Iqbal Qaiser from taking photographs. But he continued to do so as soon as the man left.

'Please introduce yourselves,' said the police official after following us for a little while. It is for moments like these that I carry my press card, a convenient escape from all inconvenient situations. Satisfied, the policeman left us to ourselves.

Walking over to a small room behind the shrine, I joined a couple of dervishes engaged in a religious discussion. One of them sat behind a boiling pot of *kawa* that he offered to devotees. The room grew awkwardly silent.

'I write books. Can you tell me a bit about the saint?' I asked.

'What books have you written?'

'It's an English book yet to be published,' I replied trying to put an end to the conversation that took place in Punjabi.

'What is the name of the book?'

'Well it's not decided as yet.'

'What is this notebook you are carrying with you? Show me,' one dervish said.

I handed him the book doubting his ability to read my notes in English. 'Peacocks. Mickey Mouse. Pakistan.' I knew he was avoiding the difficult words: institutionalization, commercialization, Americanization. What was he doing, I wondered. Was he trying to impress me? Trying to raise his status in front of me by exhibiting his ability to read English? He kept turning the pages, loudly reading out bits and pieces from my notes. With every page he turned, my temper rose. 'India. Multan. Dogs.'

In that moment the gravity of the situation dawned upon me. These were my notes, including a critique of religious practices I had witnessed. And I am still in a country that is becoming increasingly religiously intolerant. I thought about the case of a dentist from Karachi accused of blasphemy and now languishing in jail for throwing a business card of a salesman into the dustbin. The name of the salesman was Muhammad. I thought about the businessman from Kasur who was lynched by his own factory workers for taking off an outdated calendar from his wall and placing it on the floor. The calendar contained verses from the Quran. Stroking his white beard the dervish concentrated hard on the pages and occasionally smiled as if he had found what he was looking for.

'Why are you going through my notes? These are personal. I came here to seek your help and this is what you are doing?

Tell me if you want to help me otherwise I'll just go but give me back my notebook,' I shouted at him.

The other dervish cooking *kawa* also exhorted him to return the book.

'Why are you getting scared? I am no IS [he meant ISI-Inter-Services Intelligence] or FA [FIA-Federal Investigation Agency].'

'I don't care who you are or are not. But you can't do this. You've started reading from the start. What are you looking for?'

Embarrassed at being shouted at in front of other devotees, he handed the notebook back to me. Maybe he was from the ISI, I thought, dressed up as a dervish. Only a week ago, a blast at the shrine of Pir Hajan Shah Huzoori at the village of Marri near Shikarpur, Sindh, had killed four people and injured several others. All the major shrines of the country, including this one, were on high alert. It is for this reason that the police and Auqaf Department officials were forbidding us from taking photographs.

Still irritated, I asked the other dervish, who was seventy-five years old and named Ghulam Muhammad, a few questions about the shrine.

'How long have you been here?'

'He won't answer that,' replied the 'IS' dervish, Muhammad Aslam.

'Ask me something about the saint, not myself,' said Ghulam Muhammad.

'Why did the saint have so many crows?'

'That question was once posed to Kawan Wali Sarkar. He replied that crows have long lives. "Maybe one of these crows has seen the Holy Prophet (PBUH). In serving these crows

I am serving the Prophet," he replied.'

Crows do not have long lives, at least no longer than humans. However, the reference being made here is to the ancient Hindu belief that crows are a bridge between the living and the dead. In traditional Hindu homes, crows are offered a handful of rice before any meal. This is regarded as akin to feeding one's ancestors.[81]

Using hyperbole and fancy vocabulary, Muhammad Aslam explained again what Ghulam Muhammad said. This added to my suspicion. Did he even know anything about the shrine?

Kawan Wali Sarkar's real name was Karam Ilahi and he was born in the year 1838. We do not know if he was a Syed or a descendant of the Prophet, but his spiritual master, Syed Imaam Shah Qadri, was one for sure. Kawan Wali died in the year 1929, years before the Pakistan movement was to have any serious ramifications on the politics and religion of united India. He was a malamati peer, who undermined his spiritual prowess by his eccentric behaviour and by debasing himself. During his lifetime, he must have regularly interacted with Hindu sadhus and yogis learning about Hindu mythology and tradition. If he was not a descendant of the Prophet by familial connections, he, like other Muslims, thought of himself as a spiritual descendant of the Prophet. Therefore, feeding the crows became for him a symbolic gesture to seek the blessings of the Prophet of Islam, a tradition that he clearly picked up from Hindu mythology, giving it his own flavour.

'Is that the picture of the saint?' I asked pointing towards a black and white picture hung on a wall behind Ghulam Muhammad. It depicted the saint sitting in the middle, surrounded by crows and a few men at some distance. This was also the posture depicted in his posters. He seemed almost in rage while staring at the camera.

'He would not allow humans to come too close to him, often cursing at them to stay away,' said Muhammad Aslam.

Amazed at the resilience of his devotees, I wondered why they would choose to stay on even after being told to leave him alone.

'Why would the saint do that?' I asked.

'Because of his spirituality. He would get angry. He was a malamati, which means he did not conform to the laws of the Shariah. The Shariah scholars did not like him. They never understood him really. After his death all the maulvis refused to offer his *namaz-e-jinnazah*. His funeral prayer was then led by Peer Waliyat Shah. He told all the other scholars that he had seen Kawan Wali Sarkar at Kaaba and they don't know his real status.'

'What religious sect did Peer Waliyat belong to?'

'Naqshbandi,' was the reply.

This was unexpected. Along with the Deoband, Naqshbandis are considered to be the most puritanical in their religious outlook, and here was this orthodox scholar paying his tribute to a malamati.

'All langar provided to devotees at the shrine is offered to the crows before anybody else. Children who stutter or have other speaking problems drink water from the same vessel as the crows and are cured. This ash here is also sacred,' said Ghulam Muhammad, picking a little from under the pot. 'Devotees eat it and all their problems are solved.'

'Would the saint light his fire here?'

'Occasionally, he would do it whenever he felt like it. But

he slept in that room,' he said, pointing to a door behind a few female devotees.

'Once a woman came to the *kawan wali sarkar* and asked for water from his vessel. "Go have water from that well," he said. "It's not like that well has milk," the woman replied. "It has milk now," replied the saint and when the woman got to the well it actually had milk.'

'Where is the well?'

'Behind this room.'

'Does it still have milk?'

'No. It finished during the governance of the British,' explained Ghulam Muhammad but did not give any details.

'Allama Iqbal also once came to see the saint. One of his devotees told him that the Allama wants to speak to him. "All of them are Allamas for me," replied the saint referring to his crows.'

'Please forgive me if I have offended you,' apologized Muhammad Aslam as I got up to leave.

'Please excuse me for my outburst as well,' I said feeling bad about losing my temper.

'You should have never given the notebook to him,' said Iqbal Qaiser later in the car while we were driving back to Lahore. 'But forget about it now. Do you know that Gujrat became an important city during the tenure of Akbar? Before that it was a small village. One of Akbar's wives is also buried here.'

≈

'That's really interesting. A shrine of sacred dogs!' said Sarfraz Ansari, a veteran theatre actor, with excitement. 'You should make a documentary on all these shrines associated with animals. The shrine of dogs, of cats.'

'Excuse me? Did you just say shrine of cats.'

'Yes. Haven't you seen it? It's next to Bhatti gate. It's called Billiyon Wala Mazaar.'

A few days later, accompanied by a photographer friend, Samra Noori, I headed towards the walled city of Lahore, of which Bhatti gate is one of the twelve entry points. The shrine was a tall single-storey structure embedded into a curve of the street. Its tall minarets highlighted the transition that the shrine was going through, from being a syncretistic Sufi shrine to a monolithic mosque—a transition that we later found out was almost complete. 'Hazrat Baba Ghulam Rasool Biliyan wali sarkar,' read the inscription at the entrance. Like *kutiyan wali,* and *kawan wali,* the saint here was *billiyan wali* as opposed to *billiyan wala,* which in Urdu would generally be used for a male while wali is used for females. However, given the Sufi tradition of referring to oneself as a female in a relationship with God, all these saints had become *wali* from *wala.*

The grave of the saint, which recorded his year of death as 1973, was located in a corner of the small building. A major part of the shrine had been occupied by a mosque that must have come up here after the establishment of the shrine. Near the entrance was a pot, containing milk, surrounded by ruffled up kittens. Some had injury marks. A few, reasonably healthy ones, drank the milk, while a couple lay vulnerably amongst the shoes of the devotees. Within the recess of the wall was a wooden cabinet which I opened to find several kittens clinging to each other. They all looked sick or physically injured. I stepped into the mosque to find young devotees sleeping in the cool room, a comfortable spot on this July afternoon. The only person I could approach sitting next to the grave, was a mute who was kind enough to go out and bring back forty-year-old Muhammad Tanveer, an old devotee of the shrine.

'The saint loved cats,' he said. 'He would feed them milk and food, so they would always surround him. Earlier there used to be several more, but now their numbers have dwindled. This is because we don't encourage the practice anymore. These kittens enter the mosque and spoil the holy space. People drop off their unwanted kittens here, but we really wish they wouldn't.'

Tanveer took us outside to show us the writing next to the entrance. 'It is forbidden to drop off kittens here. But that still doesn't discourage people. The problem is that there is no one at the shrine to take care of the cats. They venture out on the main road and become victims of road accidents. Look at that one for example,' he said pointing to a disabled kitten taking refuge under a watermelon cart in front of the shrine. 'She will die soon. This is brutal. We cannot let this happen for long. So many times have we picked them up and dropped them off at empty plots but somehow new ones come.'

Cats as opposed to dogs have traditionally been favoured as pets by Muslims. Abu-Hurayra, one of the companions of the Prophet, was given this title which means Father of a Kitten, by the Prophet, because he was always accompanied by a female cat.[82] It is believed that the Prophet also had a pet cat called Muizza. It is reported that the Prophet used to cut off the sleeve of his shirt to get up for prayers instead of disturbing the cat sleeping on it. Several Hadiths depict the Prophet's fondness for cats—he is said to allow Muslims to eat food that cats have sampled or perform ablution from water from which they have drunk.[83] In the Islamic mystical tradition, several orders, including the Siddi Haddi and the Mevlevis, are known for their affection for cats. Hundreds of cats are fed and cared for in their lodges and even given human names.[84]

About a year after my trip to the shrine of cats, Samra Noori returned there without me. 'Haroon, there aren't any kittens there anymore,' she told me over the phone. This was not unexpected given that the caretakers at the shrine were eager to purge the shrine of the kittens. The fact that the shrine is located in the heart of Lahore, a major metropolitan city, is probably why this practice has diminished much faster than it would have in a more peripheral location.

As other cities and villages where these shrines are based get absorbed into the larger socio-economic structure of the global economy, they tend to shed their idiosyncrasies, eager to conform to the universally understood concepts of religiosity.

# 7
# Syncretism in the Mainstream

SO FAR, READING the book, one may get the impression that
religious syncretism is a phenomenon that has only survived
in rural Pakistan. This notion is not wholly correct. On peeling
away the surface of several religious practices in cities, one
would come across surprising stories of religious sharing,
reflective of a fluidity that existed between the different
religions of pre-Partition India. In this chapter, I aim to discuss
two such schools of thought, dominant in the major cities of
the country and very much part of the mainstream religion,
which have been borne out of, and became popular primarily
because of their religious syncretism.

≈

I was only ten when I first took part in the celebration of Eid
Milad-Un-Nabi. Some older boys from my mohalla spent the
entire day collecting mud from their surroundings, gathering
it at one corner, and making a small *pahari* (mound). As all
the children chipped in, bringing their toys—the writhing

G.I. Joe, the bicycle kid who would go round and round in circles, the mechanical Ken and Barbie shaking their legs and hands to the pathetic music of the early nineties—I brought my red tape recorder which played the famous Arabic song 'Didi'. As a child everything in Arabic was sacred to me, and what could be more appropriate on this day than this song?

'What are you doing this for?' I asked Irfan, one of the older kids, referring to the preparations.

'It's for our Holy Prophet (PBUH). Today is his birthday,' he replied.

'What is this *pahari* for?' I persisted with my questions.

'It represents the mountain where the Prophet used to go to meditate: the cave of Hira, where he received the first message of Islam.'

Even as a child I knew that the G.I Joe writhing outside the symbolic cave was an anomaly. Barbie in her dress that revealed her legs was inappropriate as well, given the sanctity of the place, but Irfan was older than me. So I let this historical inaccuracy pass.

'It's a good effort, but the boys at the mohalla nearby have done a better job with their mound,' said a boy who had come to visit us on his red bike.

'Shove it,' replied Irfan.

In present day, about twenty years later, the pomp and fair with which the birthday of the Prophet is celebrated has increased. A couple of years ago, on the eve of the celebration, I visited a mohalla called Khadak. Its narrow lanes were decorated with fairy lights and colourful tents. Several roads had been blocked off for cars and bikes, the space taken over by the boys and young men from the community to decorate their *paharis*.

'We've spent one and a half lakh rupees on the arrangement,' said Yasin, a peon at my father's factory—Yasin's income was only 7,000 rupees per month. In front of us were large replicas of the Kaaba and Masjid Nabwi, while in the centre was an elaborate fish-shaped structure, which I later found out was the symbolic shoe of the Prophet, heralding his arrival into the world to put a permanent end to the era of ignorance—one so gruesome that it can only be defined by the Arabic word jahillay, the English rendition failing to do justice to the ignominy that such ignorance carries. This shoe is the symbol of the festival of Eid Milad-Un-Nabi, and flags and stickers featuring it are now a popular adornment on houses and autorickshaws.

'Where did you get that money from?' I asked Yasin.

'Everyone contributed. The entire mohalla. Did you see Arsalan's decorations on the way? Are ours better or his?'

Pretending to think about the question, I said, 'Yours.'

A couple of streets away, Arsalan, another worker from the factory, had raised a *pahari* made out of pebbles. Water oozed out from its centre, forming a thick layer of froth on top. Eid Milad-Un-Nabi marks the birthday of the Prophet. However, according to tradition it also marks the day that he died. Followers of the Ahle-Hadith, Deoband and other puritanical schools of thought maintain that the day should be commemorated with sobriety instead of celebration. It is not celebrated anywhere in the Middle East, they argue. On the other hand, the Barelvis, an offshoot of the Deoband School, maintain that the day should be celebrated instead of mourned.

After separating from the Deoband in the nineteenth century, and spearheaded by Ahmed Raza Khan, the Barelvis embraced folk religious practices. The majority of Muslims in India and Pakistan belong to this particular school of thought. Differences between the two sects originated over an argument on the status of the Prophet. The Deobands maintain that the Prophet, like all other humans, was an ordinary individual who received divine guidance. The Barelvis believe that he was not an ordinary human being but was special even before he became a Prophet, having been created out of divine radiance. The Barelvis in Pakistan have taken a clear stance against the Talibanization of society, condemning their interpretation of religion. The Deobands, on the other hand, have failed to denounce Islamic religious terrorism in the same manner.

Eid Milad-Un-Nabi is a national holiday and boys and young men spend several days preparing their *paharis* for an unofficial competition. Processions and rallies are held all over the country, with hymns sung in praise of the Prophet. In upper-class localities where the enthusiasm and the commitment to partake in such elaborate decorations are missing, houses are lit and flags raised to pledge their loyalty to the cause.

Over the past few years, the scale of the festivities has increased. Whereas earlier it was considered a pariah religious festival, even referred to as a fake Eid by many, now it has become a mainstream festival. Those who would earlier just offer a few prayers and distribute eatables to neighbours, now raise flags. Those who raised flags now put up lights. Those who lit lights now have their own *paharis*. This increase in fervour, I believe, is in reaction to the increase of religious puritanism. Those whose daily lives have been affected by the acts of violence perpetuated in the name of religion have not reacted by abandoning the faith, but by embracing an interpretation that is tolerant and syncretistic, allowing for non-Muslims to take part as well.

What is more interesting is not the festival itself but its inception. Hardly anyone knows that this festival was originally inspired by a Hindu festival called Ram Navami. The festival celebrates the birth of Ram, a popular deity, and several processions, meetings and prayers are organized by his devotees to mark the occasion. Streets are lit and the entire community takes part in the festivities, similar to the way young Muslim boys celebrate the occasion of Eid Milad-Un-Nabi. Hindus have been celebrating Ram Navami for centuries, while Muslims have been celebrating Eid Milad-Un-Nabi for about seven decades.

In 1935, a group of about a hundred people left the premises of the historical Wazir Khan Mosque, constructed in the seventeenth century by Wazir Khan, Mughal Emperor Shahjahan's governor of Lahore, singing praises in honour of the Prophet of Islam.[85] Walking around the alleys of the walled city, this group must have attracted a crowd of people, for whom this was an alien sight. Never before had anything like this been seen.

'If the Hindus can arrange festivals and hold processions for their fake gods then can't we, the inheritors of the true religion of Islam, do the same for our Prophet [PBUH],' said the prayer leader of the mosque, Maulana Syed Dedar Shah, kissing his thumbs and touching his eyes every time the name of Muhammad (PBUH) was uttered.[86]

Most of his followers rejected his idea, calling it an unlawful extension of Islam. The Deobands, who by now had established themselves as a formidable religious force in the city, opposed the idea with all their might. The average uneducated Muslim, for whom the nuances of the doctrinal differences were too profound to comprehend, was confused.

'Would it be unIslamic if I celebrated Eid Milad-Un-Nabi, the day that the Prophet also died, or should I take part in the procession and show these Hindus that we too can celebrate the birth of our Prophet?' was the conflict that haunted the average Muslim mind.

After taking a few rounds of the streets, the procession returned to the mosque. The maulana was happy with the response, and the seed for what was eventually to become one of the largest Muslim festivals of Pakistan, was sown.

Curiosity for the event increased, and ways of celebrating it became a household discussion every year. Soon after a man called Karam Elahi, also a resident of Lahore, organized his own little procession on Eid Milad-Un-Nabi, which he then merged into the Imaam's. Inayatullah Qadri, another religious scholar, started holding an annual Mehafal-e-Millad on the occasion, and on its conclusion he would lead a procession and join the group from Wazir Khan. Over the years, the popularity of the event crossed the boundaries of the walled city and spread to neighbouring villages and towns. People started decorating bull carts, camels, horses, etc., to celebrate the birthday of their beloved Prophet. The procession eventually became so big that it could no longer fill the narrow lanes of the city, and had to be moved outside Delhi Gate, where a permanent platform was constructed. Here religious orators addressed the crowd. The junction where the procession converged every year got the name of Millad Chowk. After the creation of Pakistan, the event continued to be celebrated without the government's support. In the 1980s, however, when the military dictator, General Zia-ul-Haq, undertook the process of Islamization, he also recognized the festival and for the first time Eid Milad-Un-Nabi was celebrated at the government level, which helped it gain popularity throughout the country.

While the fervour with which this festival is celebrated has increased, its opposition from puritanical schools of thought has also increased. Almost every year processions in one city or the other are marred by sectarian conflict. This remains a problem particularly in cities like Sargodha, Faisalabad and Dera Ismael Khan, where ultra-orthodox Sunni organizations have a large support base. Although until now these incidents have been minor, and no major conflict has erupted, celebrations for Eid Milad-Un-Nabi are gaining momentum and are increasingly being supported by people who seem to be tired of a spartan religion that is promoted by orthodox schools of thought.

This festival that brings together music, dance, festivities, and other features, is South Asian in its essence and an example of the syncretistic tradition that Pakistani Islam is a product of.

≈

I waited outside the small makeshift room covered by curtains. This is where women were checked by female police officials. I could hear an argument from within and knew that it was the police officials insisting that Maryam drop her camera there and pick it up on her way back. After a little while she along with Anam and a stern-looking police official emerged. Maryam pointed towards me. I was directed to the head of security to whom I showed my press card and told that we had driven here from Lahore, a journey of about four hours, to do a piece on the shrine of Baba Farid and that we needed photographs for the article. Attacks against shrines were becoming frequent and hence the new security protocols. A couple of years prior to our visit there was a blast at the entrance of the shrine killing six people. In March 2009 the popular shrine of Rahman Baba was attacked in Peshawar resulting in the death of over 100 people. On 3 April 2011 the shrine of Sakhi Sarwar in Dera Ghazi Khan was bombed killing around fifty people. On 1 July 2010 three bomb blasts rocked the most important shrine of Lahore, Data Darbar, resulting in the death of five people and injuring more than hundred and seventy-five. On 6 October 2010 the shrine of Abdullah Shah Ghazi in Karachi was attacked killing eight people.

Ever since the inception of such syncretistic shrines they have been criticized by orthodoxy. Intellectual battles have been fought for several years but never before have they been physically attacked. Despite religious differences the sanctity of these shrines has always been respected and whoever has sought refuge within such spaces has been granted so. However, that had changed. These spaces of protection were themselves under attack. This was a new phenomenon.

Photography was strictly prohibited in all such shrines following the attacks. There were elaborate security measures at the entrance. Earlier these shrines would remain open throughout the night providing shelter to all, but now they are shut at midnight on the order of the government.

Looking at my press card, the head of the security arrangement allowed us to take the cameras inside the shrine and take photographs. The shrine of Baba Farid is located on the top of a mound that overlooks the entire city. There is always a rush outside the shrine, where there are several shops selling religious paraphernalia. It is considered inauspicious to visit the grave of a saint without a gift. From these shops devotees buy chaddar, flowers and incense sticks to be presented to the caretakers of the shrine. It seems as if the entire city of Pakpattan has developed around this shrine. All roads lead here. The name of every other shop or business entity either includes Baba Farid or his title Ganj Shakar (Treasure of Sugar). There are several myths as to how the saint earned this title—one of them being that he was extremely soft-spoken.

The city of Pakpattan was a small, insignificant one known as Ajodhan on the bank of river Sutlej when Baba Farid had decided to settle here in the thirteenth century. He was at that point the head of Chisti order with its centre in Delhi. Baba Farid had believed that the religious order should distance itself from the imperial authority hence he had shifted the centre from Delhi to Ajodhan. The madrassah of Baba Farid was located on the mound where he is buried.

We climbed the stairs and found ourselves in an open courtyard with a new mosque on one side and the shrine of Baba Farid in front of us. There was a huge line of men eagerly waiting to be ushered into the shrine of the Sufi saint. Women are not allowed inside the chamber where the grave is located. For them there is a verandah adjacent to the shrine, from where they can catch a glimpse of the grave. This was a modest building. Behind the shrine is a splendid structure rising several metres higher. This is where the progeny of Baba Farid is buried. The graves of his female family members are covered with purdah. Here too women are not allowed. Comparing these two buildings one can see the transition that occurred after the death of Baba Farid, who had lived a life of poverty and away from the politics of his time. His progeny benefitted from the legacy of the saint and received gifts and awards from different rulers. The current guardians of the shrine are from the family of Baba Farid and they are not only one of the richest but also one of the most powerful families of the region.

Facing the shrine is an ancient Karir tree. It is about this tree that a disciple of Baba Farid, Nizamuddin Auliya wrote. He stated that the day *dela*, an unripe fruit of the wild Karir tree, was cooked it was regarded as a feast by the students. Nizamuddin Auliya became the head of the Chisti order after Baba Farid and moved back the madrassah to Delhi. He is buried there and his shrine attracts thousands of Hindus, Muslims and Sikhs every day.

The Chisti order was introduced in India by Moinuddin Chisti in the twelfth century. He is buried in Ajmer, Rajasthan, where his shrine too has become the site of a major pilgrimage. The order was founded in the tenth century in a small city called Chist, presently in Afghanistan. The Chisti order is today one of the most popular Sufi orders in India and Pakistan.

What made the Chisti order so popular in this part of the world is its openness to all religious traditions and practices. It allowed influences from other religions to be incorporated into its order. One of them is qawwali, which has its origin in the ancient devotional musical traditions of India, primarily bhajan. Qawwalis are now a prominent feature of all Chisti shrines. Kirtan, the devotional Sikh music which developed a few centuries later, has uncanny similarities to qawwali. At the shrine of Baba Farid, the most important Chisti Sufi in Pakistan, there are qawwals performing at all times of the day.

Sitting under the shade of a building across from the Karir tree was a group of qawwals. There was one man on the harmonium and one on tabla while the rest of them clapped along and provided background vocals. Qawwali like jazz is improvised music. Using a main line and tune the musicians improvise adding verses from various Sufi poets. Aptly the musicians were singing verses of Baba Farid. Behind the qawwals was the langar hall, offering free food to all. This tradition too was introduced to Sufi shrines by the Chisti order.

Perhaps the greatest contribution of Baba Farid is not in religion but in literature. He is believed to be the first poet of Punjabi. He became an inspiration for Guru Nanak when he visited the shrine during his travels. Here through the descendants of Farid he learned about the poetry of Baba Farid. It is through this path that eventually the poetry of Baba Farid found its way into the Guru Granth Sahib, making Baba Farid a saint in Sikh tradition as well. For years now Sikhs have petitioned the Pakistani government to grant them visas to attend the *urs* of Baba Farid but in vain. There is a picture of Baba Farid accompanying the picture of Guru Nanak at the shrine of Guru Nanak at Nankana Sahib.

We sat facing the qawwals along with several other pilgrims. After a little while a young man, wearing an off-white shalwar kameez, started whirling on his knees in a state of trance. The qawwals continued singing passionately. Another devotee threw notes of ten rupees in the air which one of the assistants of the qawwals collected and put in front of him. Here women and men sat together. After about half-an-hour later drenched in sweat the qawwals were replaced by another group in their crispy shalwar kameez.

Qawwali at Sufi shrines is one of the main causes of irritants to the orthodoxy who maintain that music is un-Islamic. Talking about the role of the Sufi saints like Baba Farid they argue that they condoned qawwali at that time because they wanted to win over Hindus into Islam and since the Hindus were used to bhajans, the Muslims had to perform qawwalis. However today there is no need for qawwali. The practitioners of the art on the other hand continue regarding qawwali as a form of divine connection, allowing them to get closer to God.

While sitting at the shrine of Baba Farid, I looked around to see the group of devotees gathered here. Judging by their clothes I could tell that they belonged to different socio-economic backgrounds. I wondered how many of them were regular visitors to the shrine? Was any one of them present when the shrine was attacked? Did the attack scare them or did the passion of the devotee increase after the attack? I grappled with all these questions as I saw several more devotees around me slip into a state of trance.

≈

8

# The Two-nation Theory

'WHAT IS THE opposite of Islam?' I asked my fourteen-year-old students during a world history class. The discussion had somehow diverted to the topic of Islam. Eager hands rose into the air calling for my attention.

'It's Hinduism,' one student said. All the students agreed.

'Would that also hold true for Muslims in, let's say, Egypt?' I followed up with another question, enjoying the process.

'There it would be Christianity.'

'No. Judaism,' said another boy.

There was uncertainty in trying to identify a universal antonym for Islam; however, in the Pakistani context, a consensus on Hinduism was easy to establish. I do not know if my question was a valid one. Would it be possible to define a religion with its antonym? However, my purpose in posing this question to the students was not to determine the opposite, a futile exercise in itself, but to peek into their minds and try to understand how they understood Islam, Hinduism and the Pakistani nationalism premised around it. Their confusion in dealing with the question indicated that a religion perhaps cannot be defined in opposition to another religion. But in Pakistan this can be done so easily.

Carved out of India in 1947 on the basis of the two-nation theory, the raison d'être for Pakistan is its opposition to India, a Hindu majority nation. That Hindus and Muslims are separate entities based on their different and opposing religions, culture, history and language, is the lifeline of the theory. School textbooks on Pakistan Studies highlight that India was a land lost in the darkness of ignorance, where a beacon of light arrived with the Muslims.[87] Students grow up believing that Hindus are evil because they worship several deities with several hands. They are evil because they burn widows and practice caste system. It is taught that during the Partition, Hindus killed Muslims because the Muslims wanted to live peacefully in their new homeland and the Muslims only killed Hindus and Sikhs in retaliation. Citing examples of the destruction of the Babri mosque in 1992 and the Gujarat Muslim killings of 2002, students in schools and colleges are made to believe that Hindus are not capable of living together with Muslims, and that they, the students, have been lucky to be blessed with Pakistan otherwise they would have been subjected to slavery by Hindus.

Pakistan Studies, a subject that replaced History and is compulsory for all school and college students, begins with the Indus Valley Civilization, and goes on to discuss Buddhism and then the first Muslim invasion of Muhammad bin Qasim, leaving a vacuum of more than a millennium when Hindu kingdoms dominated this land. In the nationalistic discourse, all traces of the Hindu past are obliterated because of the fear that they might dilute the Pakistani identity. Thousands of years of history and culture are reinterpreted to highlight the differences between Muslims and Hindus, Pakistanis and Indians. For example: 'They worship cows, we sacrifice them. They worship idols, we shatter them. Their villains are our heroes.'

Muslim invaders of India, from Muhammad bin Qasim to Ahmad Shah Abdali, are celebrated in the Pakistani historiography as Islamic warriors who fought to spread the message of Islam. The nuances of political motivations and greed are stripped off from these characters and their battles are depicted as those between good and evil, between Muslims and Hindus. The nuclear warheads of Pakistan are named after Ahmad Shah Abdali, Mahmud Ghazni, Mohammad Ghori and Babur, to celebrate their conquests. In contrast to them, the local rulers who fought against the invaders are depicted as villains of Pakistan.

The fact that some of the invaders fought against fellow Muslim rivals and in the process eliminated cities and villages which had a Muslim populace, along with Hindus and Sikhs, is conveniently swept under the carpet. I have gotten into several arguments with my friends, educated at the same school and university as me, over the role of Muslim invaders like Muhammad Ghori and Ahmad Shah Abdali. For them they are no less than holy warriors whose only motivation was the dissemination of Islam, greed playing no role in their conquests. The fact that the Somnath temple that Muhammad Ghori had pillaged and destroyed was also one of the richest temples in India, is regarded as a mere coincidence.

A few years ago, when I was working at an elite school in Lahore, one that has more than a hundred branches all over the country, I came across a poster in the corridor captioned 'Muslim heroes'. The poster had photographs of Muhammad bin Qasim, Mahmud Ghazni and Ahmad Shah Abdali. Walking back I wondered why our heroes cannot be people like Baba Farid, Waris Shah and Bulleh Shah, who spread the message of peace and brought several religious communities together instead of shedding blood. Being fed on propaganda like this allows for the creation of an environment in the country in which there are divisions based on religious identities—Muslims and non-Muslims—with the latter being tolerated by the community instead of being embraced. Incidents of violence against minorities breed in such an atmosphere of separateness.

Having strict notions of what it means to be a Muslim, defined as something that is not Hindu or Sikh, the educated people in the country, who are part of the elite, have reinterpreted Islamic religious practices, adopting sects and schools of thought that are more puritanical in nature. They believe Sufi shrines and religious traditions that are inspired by non-Muslim practices, or are syncretistic, are impure and need to be shunned. It is primarily for these reasons that shrines which are located in developed areas, where people are more educated, are losing their idiosyncrasies much faster than those found in remote regions. Given these circumstances, it would be safe to say that Muslim fundamentalism (not defined as militancy but puritanism) is more popular in the urban centres compared to the rural.

Growing up in this environment, I was no different from the average Pakistani student who thought of Indians as others and believed that we as Muslims and Pakistanis were everything the Indians were not. It was only when I started exploring the folk religion of the country that I began to fully understand the issues at hand. I was fascinated by Pakistan's non-Muslim heritage, but for me it was separate from my heritage. Through these shrines I began to understand that at a folk level, where the primordial identity of a society is not tinged by nationalistic fervour and religious puritanism, these distinct boundaries do not really exist. Given that most of these practices and shrines developed over thousands of years, borrowing and adopting from different religious sources, such syncretism is not extraordinary per se. For the longest period in history, interaction between different villages and cities remained limited because of hostile routes and no other medium of communication. Therefore, when Islam was introduced to people here, it was understood in a language that was already available to the locals through existing religious practices. Throughout the time that communication remained limited, such practices thrived, reconfiguring old traditions and mixing up new ones to present something unique in their own regard.

However, that changed after the creation of Pakistan, built on the concept of its exclusivity from Hinduism. In the changing atmosphere, these syncretistic practices found themselves in a precarious place defying the exclusive separatist nationalism. It is primarily for this reason that such idiosyncratic shrines become extraordinary, a repository of tradition that is no longer acceptable, yet prevalent throughout the country. In other words, the shrines are extraordinary because they continue to survive in an environment constructed out of Muslim separatism.

While this syncretism fascinates me, its impure past attracts the wrath of the religious and nationalist puritans. Earlier this threat came in the form of 'education' and 'development' but now it is physical with the rise of Islamic militancy. Over the years, several such Sufi shrines have been bombed by militants, as they hurt their religious sensibilities. The elite, who do not present a physical danger to the militants, however, look down upon such practices believed to be not reflective of 'pure Islam'. I remember a couple of years ago, I was sitting across from a panel of educated Pakistanis being interviewed for a foreign scholarship. During the course of the interview, a discussion on the culture of Pakistan emerged. In order to impress the interviewers I told them about the shrines of phallic offerings.

'But that's not true Islam,' said one of the women on the panel.

'What is then?' I asked her. 'That which is followed in Saudi Arabia, or which is followed by the Taliban, or that which is practised in Iran?'

'That which is mentioned in the Quran and the Sunnah,' she argued.

'All of them draw their legitimacy from the Quran,' I replied.

A few weeks later I received a rejection letter for the scholarship.

The Pakistani education system is devoid of any cultural and historical understanding of the region, as it is a legacy of the colonial state apparatus. Therefore it can be argued that the education system is not rooted in the cultural and historical ethos of the country.

Pakistan Studies on the other hand, serves the purpose of nationalistic propaganda. The repercussions of this, at an intellectual level, can be discussed in volumes. But there is also a practical incentive in instructing future generations in the local culture and history. Children who are a product of this education system grow up with undefined notions of identity, something that can be rectified with a historical understanding. It is this vacuum which is then exploited by religious demagogues giving people a false sense of identity, of 'Islamic roots'. This phenomenon explains the rise of religious intolerance in Pakistani society. Such shrines and traditional practices should not only be preserved for the sake of religious pluralism but for maintaining the social fabric of society which is being torn apart by Islamic militancy. However, at the moment, the biggest threat to the shrines doesn't come from militancy but rather from education and development.

# 9

## The Counter-narrative

AHMAD SHAH DURRANI (1747–1772), an Afghan ruler, is considered to be a national hero in Pakistan historiography. However a small shrine in the outskirts of Lahore raised by the villagers there tell a different story. The narrative of the state and the narrative of the people diverge here.

≈

When talks began between the Sikh insurgents and representatives of the governor, there were hopes that years of violence would finally come to an end. Ever since the fall of the Mughal Empire conditions had deteriorated in Punjab. Ahmad Shah Abali, the Afghan king, had already completed two raids of Punjab and beyond, and was planning a third one. Moin-ul-Mulk, popularly known as Meer Manu, was the governor of Punjab and besides warding off yet another attack by Ahmad Shah Abdali he was also constantly pestered by the Sikh insurgent groups Misl, which had sprung up all over Punjab. The most powerful of the Sikh group was

Khalsa Dal, headed by Jassa Singh Kalal based near Amritsar. The Sikh groups did not control much land but because of their anti-status quo politics the lower rungs of the society supported and protected them. Meer Manu was aware of the increasing sympathy that the Sikh groups were garnering and knew that if he had to root out their insurgency he would have to turn them into villains in the popular imagination. Hence using the state machinery he cast the battle between the state and insurgents as a war between Muslims and Sikhs, even though there were several Muslims in the Sikh groups and many non-Muslim soldiers in the army of Meer Manu. This had its desired effect and the reputation of the Sikh forces began to suffer. In this state of vulnerability they accepted the government's offer of negotiation.

From the governor's side it was Raja Kaura Mal, his trusted Hindu minister who was heading the talks. Initially violence subsided and it seemed as if the talks would yield result. But as negotiations dragged on, the forces of the governor became impatient and attacked a few Sikh villages. It was impossible to continue talks after these attacks and the Sikh insurgents once again raised their heads.

It was in this environment that Ahmad Shah Abdali was planning his third attack. After his first attack Ahmad Shah and agreed an annual tax stipulation which the governor was responsible of paying to him, for the right of governing Punjab. A couple of years ago when Meer Manu failed to pay the required amount Ahmad Shah crossed the river Indus causing havoc in all the cities and villages that fell on the way. Before Ahmad Shah could reach Lahore, the prize possession of Punjab, Meer Manu met him at a place near the city of Gujrat and averted the disaster by agreeing to pay the stipulated amount. This year as well the situation was similar and Ahmad Shah had crossed Indus destroying everything in his way. The governor believed that he would cross the path of the Afghan King before he could enter Lahore and once again avert the disaster. Ahmad Shah this time had every intention of capturing Lahore, so he marched further north bypassing the governor, who was waiting for him near Gujrat.

Unhindered, the forces of Ahmad Shah Abdali reached Lahore, and laid a siege on it. For months the citizens were trapped within the walls of their city. To keep themselves busy the forces of Ahmad Shah would attack villages and towns in the outskirt of Lahore. This also allowed them to replenish their stock. On one of these days while Ahmad Shah was encamped outside of Lahore an informant from within the city reached his camp. He told him that a few kilometres from Lahore there was a prosperous village called Maraka, occupied by Sikh insurgents, who had grown rich by attacking Muslim villages. To avenge the 'honour' of Muslims Ahmad Shah headed south to capture the Sikh leaders of Maraka.

≈

Pointing at the blackened surface of a brick, Iqbal Qaiser told me that the village was burned. There were several bricks and relics of pottery scattered all over the graveyard. Some of the bricks were in clusters, damaged by the heat of the raging fire. After the entire population of this small village had been wiped out, the houses were subjected to arson. History books might be influenced by ideological considerations but this abandoned mound, a few kilometres inroad from the

Multan Road highway, is testimony to the atrocities of the forces of Ahmad Shah Abdali. Iqbal Qaiser picked up one of the bricks and put it in the car's trunk for his private collection. There were several graves all over the mound, while on the edge an ancient banyan tree stood silently, holding within the screams of women and children as they burned in their houses. Behind it a canal flowed, seemingly weeping at the death of the innocent, struggling in vain to break through its bank to quench the thirst of the fire.

We parked our car next to the village mosque and headed towards Esaiyan da mazaar, the shrine of the Christians, hidden within the bosom of the village of Maraka. The shrine was a small structure with a single grave in the centre, and the mark of a cross at the entrance. 'This is the shrine of Baba Gur Baksh Masih,' said the forty-year-old Basheer as he handed his hash-filled cigarette to his young companions. Masih, in the name of the saint, implied that he was a Christian. Basheer's beard, white in colour, was thick, while kohl was smeared around his eyes. He lived in a makeshift room within the complex and had been looking after the shrine for the past twenty years. 'Baba Gur Baksh Masih was a follower of Guru Nanak. Once while he was fighting, his head was severed but his body continued fighting and eventually came and rested here,' Basheer told us.

'And whose graves are those?' I asked, pointing to a few mud graves under the trees behind the shrine.

'They were followers of Baba Gur Baksh Masih.'

Before our visit to the village of Maraka, Iqbal Qaiser had briefed me about its history. At the time of Partition, the majority population of the village, being Sikhs, had migrated to the safer side of the border. However, like most refugees, they too had believed that Partition was a temporary political necessity and soon they would return to their native cities and villages. With that hope the Sikhs from Maraka had left behind property and valuables, handing them over to their servants who were Mazhabi Sikhs.

Mazhabi Sikhs formerly belonged to the untouchable caste. However, their untouchability followed them into their new religion, separating them from the rest by this title. This transition even occurred in the Muslim tradition where former untouchables became Musali or Deendar. Around the time when the riots of Partition threatened to engulf this small village, these Mazhabi Sikhs removed their turbans and kirpans overnight, cut their hair and converted to Christianity, a neutral religion at that time, to avoid persecution. They have been Christians ever since. It would therefore be safe to assume that the shrine of Baba Gur Baksh Masih must have originally been the samadhi of Gur Baksh Singh, converted posthumously taking into account the changing social and political conditions. It is for this reason that Basheer said that Gur Baksh Masih was a follower of Guru Nanak.

Fascinating as it was, this shrine was not the purpose of our visit. We were looking for a shrine called Shaheedan da mazaar or the shrine of the martyred.

It so happened that when Ahmad Shah Abdali attacked this village, Bodh Singh and his son Jassa Singh, the prime targets, were away on business. On their return when they found out that their village was burned they formed a group, bringing together other victims of the wrath of the Afghan marauder, and started attacking government functionaries.

They abandoned Maraka which had become a ruin and established themselves at a place in Sialkot district. In 1797, when the grandson of Ahmad Shah Abdali, Shah Zaman Durrani, following the footsteps of his grandfather, attacked Punjab, this group of Sikh bandits, founded by Bodh Singh and now headed by his successor Nadhan Singh, met him on the banks of the Chenab, promising to help him in his raids if he returned their property in Maraka. Shah Zaman agreed. Later, during the tenure of Maharaja Ranjit Singh, this village was re-populated a few kilometres away from the ruins of the old one, now the village graveyard. It was then that a structure within the village was raised to honour the martyrs killed earlier by Ahmad Shah Abdali.

I first heard about the shrine a few years ago while visiting the ruins of this village. We had stopped at a tea shop there when an old woman approached us and enquired about the purpose of our visit. 'You should also visit the shrine of the martyrs,' she had suggested. 'In the early days, every year there used to be a small festival there, in which people danced and sang, remembering those who were martyred by the fire.'

'Did the Muslims participate in the festival?' I asked her.

'It was mainly a Christian affair but since it was such an important festival for the village, the Muslims would also participate,' she explained.

This was interesting because the Muslim population here primarily comprises people who had shifted here from India following Partition. The Christians who were indigenous to this village, had an association with the shrine and the festival, but the Muslims would not have known about its history and cultural importance in the context of the village. However, as generally happens in Pakistani villages, when a cultural event like the festival of a shrine is celebrated, everyone from the village joins in, irrespective of caste, creed and religion.

The shrine and the festival had captured my imagination particularly because it was commemorating the victims of the 1751 attack by Ahmad Shah Abdali; in other words, casting him as a villain who massacred innocent people. This was happening at the village level, while at the state level Abdali was being celebrated as a Muslim hero. It highlighted how cut off the state was from the culture and history of its own people. A national hero was a folk villain.

'Is the festival still celebrated?' I asked the old woman.

'No. But the shrine exists.'

'Who is buried within?'

'Several people, I don't know how many exactly. This village was burned once, during the time of the Hindus and when it was repopulated by the progeny of Bodh Singh, a common grave was made for all those who had died in the fire.'

I had come across the names of Bodh Singh and Jassa Singh in the book *The Punjab Chiefs* written by Lepel H. Griffin. The book records the history of this village. I was surprised to hear that the old woman had heard of him.

'Who was Bodh Singh?' I asked her.

'He was a big landlord from Maraka. When this place was burned he was away with his wife. Later they repopulated Maraka and constructed the shrine of the martyrs.'

Her version of the story that must have been transmitted orally through generations, was close to what was recorded in the book.

While I was looking at government records before

returning to Maraka to search for the shrine of the martyrs, I learned that this village was abandoned once before the attack of Ahmad Shah Abdali. According to the Land Revenue Records of 1866, Maraka was established in the latter half of the thirteenth century by a man called Marakana from Multan. The name Maraka is derived from Marakana. This, however, is part of folk history and therefore, might not be historically accurate. The record states that this village remained populated for a hundred years, attracting people from neighbouring regions because of its fertile ground. But then, almost abruptly it was abandoned due to the government's atrocities. What exactly the atrocities were, is not specified. Fifteen years later when the villagers and the government arrived at some sort of an agreement, this village was once again occupied, only to be devastated five centuries later.

'Take them to Hassan Deen's house,' Basheer commanded one of his younger companions. He knew where the shrine of the martyrs was but he was not aware of its history. We followed a young man, who dragged his feet through the labyrinth-like streets of the village.

'This is the house of Hassan Deen,' he pointed to a giant blue gate. 'Knock here and go inside,' he said before swiftly slipping away from us.

'There has been a death in the house today,' warned a shopkeeper whose shop was next to the house. We weren't sure if we would be able to see the shrine in such conditions but we were not going to leave without trying. Following the cultural tradition of entering a house uninformed where there has been a death, we entered and sat quietly for a little while with the rest of the men in the courtyard.

The occupant of the house, a seventy-eight-year-old man by the name of Muhammad Ali Cambho, agreed to show us the graves of the martyrs. Inside a circular protective wall were two simple graves, one of which was covered with an elaborate green shawl.

'Whose graves are these?' I asked our host Muhammad Ali.

'I do not know. Our family moved here at the time of Partition. We originally belong to a village near Amritsar. The shrine was already here when we moved. It was a rough structure, so we razed that and constructed these graves.'

There was no need for a samadhi in post-Partition Pakistan, so two graves were constructed instead, I thought.

'Is there a festival of the shrine?'

'Not any more. But there used to be in the early days of Pakistan.'

'Do people come to visit?'

'Not really. A few years ago a Sikh man came to see the shrine and now you have come. That's all. I don't know who the occupants of the graves are, but I still regularly clean the area and cover the graves with a shawl,' Muhammad Ali said.

I decided against telling Muhammad Ali about the history of the shrine, but as I walked back to the car I couldn't help but wonder if Muhammad Ali would still serve the graves as he did if he knew that they were raised to honour the martyrs who were massacred by a Muslim invader, regarded as a national hero.

≈

When Haji Kamal lit up a cigarette, Iqbal Qaiser, who had

stopped smoking a few years ago, was tempted. He asked for a cigarette and lit it. Sitting next to him I knew the reason for his temptation, which he later confirmed as we drove back. 'Smoking in a Sikh shrine is forbidden so I wanted to smoke.' It was a clumsy excuse, but having travelled with him for so long, I know that the forbiddance of tobacco consumption fascinates him. While we interviewed Haji Kamal, a group of devotees sat around us. I noticed an extremely old person standing at one of the four entrances. He must have been over a hundred years old. He stood frozen at the entrance for a long time, and just when I was about to get up to check on him he moved again and entered the hall. Behind me a young man had put on Waris Shah's 'Heer' on his mobile phone while a group of men was playing cards in a corner. This was a June afternoon, but the temperature inside the room was pleasant. All four entrances into the shrine, hallmark of Sikh architecture, were open and there was a breeze blowing.

'Those who have a problem with the shrine don't come. No one is forcing them to. We all come because we find solace here,' said Haji Kamal while the curious onlookers nodded in unison. Kamal had recently returned after having performed *umrah*, the lesser pilgrimage at Kaaba, and hence was being referred to as Haji by his companions.

According to the *Encyclopaedia of Sikh Literature*, this is the shrine of Sahari Mal, a disciple of the fifth Sikh guru, Guru Arjan. He was a resident of the village of Hardo Sahari, a few kilometres away from here. The shrine is located on top of a *pahari* far from civilization. The neighbouring city of Kasur is several kilometres from here.

During his lifetime, Sahari Mal had both Muslim and

Hindu followers, an ordinary tradition at that time. At Partition, the Hindus and Sikhs left, and were replaced by Muslims from Ferozepur district. Despite the changes in the socio-political conditions of the country, the indigenous Muslims of the village continued visiting the shrine, like their ancestors had for generations, irrespective of the fact that the patron saint here was not a Muslim but a Hindu (Sikhism as an institutionalized religion was not yet established). For a country formed from the Hindu and Muslim division, this is an extraordinary feat, throwing the two-nation theory topsy-turvy. Haji Kamal is a descendant of the indigenous Muslims.

'We know that Sahari Mal was a Sikh Jat but that doesn't matter to us. He was a good person and close to God,' he said.

'But over the years, attendance at the shrine has reduced,' he added, as both he and Iqbal Qaiser took a loud drag from their cigarette, flicking the ash on the floor.

A group of gypsy children, decorated with artistic designs in mud, entered the shrine to drink water from a vessel placed in one corner. Outside, there was a dried-out well, while next to it stood a huge peepal tree under which several men and women sat.

'Earlier women would bring their sick children. That was when the pool here was functional. The water in it had magical qualities and could cure all diseases,' Haji Kamal said.

The pool no longer existed and a vacant ground, surrounded by shrubs and trees, stood in its place. Colourful pieces of cloth, offerings to the shrine, were tied to some of the trees. This abandoned shrine was once popular throughout Punjab. Towards the rear of the triple-storey building with a small green dome, was a disused structure. That was the original shrine before this new building was constructed by Maharaja Ranjit Singh. As if in honour of its Sikh past, an orange flag hoisted on top of a long pole next to the shrine swayed in the hot breeze of the Punjabi summer.

'I came here a long time ago. There was a structure here made in the form of a sitting man. Where is that?' asked Iqbal Qaiser, finishing his cigarette.

'Yes, it used to exist. We have converted it into a grave. There it is,' Haji Kamal said pointing out of one door, behind which there was a simple grave, covered with a green cloth and surrounded by a few unlit lamps. This was clearly an attempt to woo conventional devotees, catering to their sensibilities.

On his deathbed, Sahari Mal had instructed his followers to neither bury him, nor cremate him because he did not want to offend the religious sensibilities of any of his devotees. Instead, he suggested that his body should be placed in a sitting yogic position and then covered. This was to be his final resting position and that is how it was for a long time till it was converted to a grave a decade ago by the Muslim devotees of the saint. Perhaps constructing a grave was a wise decision. There was no longer any question of offending the sensibilities of Hindu devotees.

'Earlier the festival of Lohri was celebrated here with much pomp and festivities. People used to sit here eating dried fruits through the cold winter nights and in the morning would travel to the shrine of Baba Ram Thamman to perform ablution,' said Haji Kamal. 'Now that tradition is over. People gather here only once a year for the annual festival in the month of Had [indigenous calendar]. A few of them visit Ram Thamman as well, while others don't.'

≈

Just a few kilometres away from the railway station of Khalu Khara, in the outskirts of the city of Kasur, is the village of Ram Thamman, named after a Hindu sadhu from the fifteenth century. According to the *Encyclopaedia of Sikh Literature*, Baba Ram Thamman was an elder cousin of Baba Guru Nanak. Ram Thamman belonged to the village of Khalu Khara, but during his lifetime settled outside the village, where his samadhi was constructed by his followers after his death. Today the complex, which includes his samadhi, Hindu temples and other historical buildings, is spread over several acres.

In pre-Partition days, the shrine of Ram Thamman used to host one of the largest festivals of Vaisakhi in Punjab, attended by Muslims, Sikhs and Hindus alike. The festival lost its allure when the Hindu and Sikh devotees of the sadhu migrated at the time of Partition and Muslim refugees took over the historical structures of the complex. One such family was that of Ghulam Hussain, who had migrated from Ferozepur.

I met Ghulam Hussain during the festival of Vaisakhi at Ram Thamman. He was eighty-five years old and full of passion. He wore a scarf around his forehead to observe the Vaisakhi festival.

'My grandfather was a sadhu here. He was living here at the time of Partition,' he said. 'As a child I came here several times.'

Forced out of his family home in Ferozepur in 1947, Ghulam Hussain's father had followed in the footsteps of his father and had come and settled here. He belonged to a large group of Muslim migrants who were in desperate search of vacant houses, temples and gurdwaras to occupy. His family had taken up the temple of Kali Mata next to the samadhi of Baba Ram Thamman. His grandfather, who had served his entire life as a sadhu here, could not allow the samadhi of his saint to be destroyed by the new occupants. So while the rest of the vacant spaces were occupied, the samadhi was kept locked by the family.

Over the years as people settled into their new homes, Ghulam Hussain's father and then Ghulam Hussain would occasionally unlock the samadhi, clean the room and change the chaddar that covered a small *pahari* which represented Baba Ram Thamman's smadh. On the occasion of Vaisakhi, while the farmers celebrated the start of their harvest season, they would open the door of the locked room in reminiscence of the days lost at the time of Partition. Over the years, as the festival of Vaisakhi revived here, so did people's devotion to the sadhu Ram Thamman. The seasonal festival once again converged with the festival of Baba Ram Thamman. Muslim groups hearing about the festivities started travelling from different parts of the country, singing and dancing on the way, presenting chaddars at the shrine, like Hindus offer chunnis at the shrine of Durga.

Selling bangles outside the shrine of the sadhu, Razzaq told me that he had been coming to the festival since he was a child.

'I used to come to the festival with my father, while he used to come with his father.'

Standing next to him, his ten-year-old-child was getting ready to keep up the family tradition.

'This is not just an economic opportunity for us, but a

religious duty,' he said.

Leading a group of dandiya dance performers, the twenty-two-year-old Ghulam Ali told me that they had come from Kasur to seek the blessings of the saint. Having offered their chaddar on a vacant charpoy, they entertained the locals with their acrobatic performance of dandiya raas, a traditional dance that is associated with Lord Krishna.

Similar to the shrine of Sahari Mal, the culture of this shrine has been upheld by local Muslim devotees of the saint; however, the nature of the festival has also been of paramount importance in making sure that the shrine is treated as holy. Celebrated at the start of the harvest season, Vaisakhi is a festival of farmers. Punjab, still predominantly an agricultural society, upholds agrarian culture and traditions, of which the harvest season is the ultimate source of happiness. However, in days following the creation of Pakistan, when an obsessive quest to define a pure Muslim culture, clean of the Hindu past, dominated the mindset of the elite of the country, several cultural festivals like Vaisakhi, Lohri and Basant were given up. 'These are not Muslim festivals but Hindu', goes the argument. As a result, several festivals which were celebrated in the early days, died an untimely death.

As 'development' slowly creeps into the areas around this abandoned village, voices against the festival of Ram Thamman are being raised. The opposition, which is negligible right now, is likely to gain fervour as Islamic fundamentalism wrapped neatly around nationalism, education and development, gains ground in remote areas. For the time being, however, the festival of Ram Thamman continues to thrive and is attended by hundreds of people every year on the occasion of Vaisakhi.

≈

Just two days after the attack on Hazara Shias in Quetta which resulted in the death of eighty-four people, Iqbal Qaiser and I visited the shrine of Sher Shah at Kahna Nau. Following the massacre of the Shias, there were nationwide protests with calls for action against the culprits, Lashkare-e-Jhangvi, a Sunni extremist organization. We were supposed to visit the shrine the day before but the road was blocked by Shia protestors.

We crossed a couple of *malangs* sitting at a table at the edge of a vacant ground which contained the shrine of the saint and a few other graves, probably of his devotees. A black flag hoisted on top of the shrine, a symbol of the Shia sect, swayed proudly. Next to it was a pole that transformed into a hand on top, as if blessing devotees. This is the Shia symbol of alm. The *malangs* looked at us sceptically while we examined the shrine and the graves around it.

'Where can we find the head of the shrine?' Iqbal Qaiser asked a devotee who was seeking the blessings of the patron saint.

'Why do you want to see him? Where are you from?' the devotee asked him.

There was tension in the air. I rolled up the sleeves of my sweater to show my collection of threads and bangles collected from the different shrines I had visited. Such religious jewellery is generally associated with the Shia sect, and people often mistake me for a Shia.

'He will come here after 1:30 p.m., but if you go to his house maybe you will find him there,' the malang guided us.

'Their house is in the gurdwara right?' asked Iqbal Qaiser.

'Yes.'

Living across the road inside an abandoned gurdwara, the progeny of the saint Sher Shah, or the King of Tigers, was the current caretaker of this Muslim shrine. The name of the gurdwara is Baba Jamiat Singh and this is what the book *Historical Sikh Shrines in Pakistan* says about it: 'Baba Jamiat Singh was a notorious thief of this area. Once, while he was getting away after stealing some buffalos, a pursuit was started. He was likely to be caught red-handed. Under the fear of apprehension he in his mind recited the name of Sat Guru and resolved not to steal again. The owner of the buffalos came close to his cattle but could not identify them. After this incident Jamiat Singh became a devotee of guru and passed his whole life reciting the name of Sat Guru. The construction work of the shrine was completed in 1921. A fair is organized every year but lacks the luster of the past.'[88]

'According to Sikh tradition, when the original owners of the cattle came across them, they failed to recognize the cattle because their patterns had changed by a miracle,' explained Iqbal Qaiser as we crossed the road heading towards the gurdwara.

'This makes for a really interesting story then. Because the Muslim shrine is associated with sacred cows, and this gurdwara, which is related to the shrine, is associated with the story of cattle,' I said in excitement, but Iqbal Qaiser ignored my comment.

'No, that's a lie,' said Shadi Shah when Iqbal Qaiser narrated the story of the gurdwara and the cattle thief to him. He was the grandson of the saint Sher Shah and the current caretaker. We were sitting inside his shop next to the gurdwara.

'But in the end, Jamiat Singh became a holy person,' ignoring Shadi's reaction, Iqbal Qaiser completed the story. Shadi's initial shock had died and he conceded that maybe such an incident could have occurred.

'How did cows become associated with the shrine of Sher Shah?' I asked Shadi.

Before coming here I had heard about this shrine and its sacred cows from various people. I had been told that the cows here are believed to be the blessed ones of the saint and are allowed to roam freely. The cows have a bag around their necks for devotees to put in money to seek their blessings.

'The Hindus and Muslims are two separate nations. They worship cows and we slaughter them,' resonated in my head while I drove to the shrine. This was one of the most popular lines justifying the need of Partition, I had heard. It used to come up in every discussion that I ever had while discussing the differences between Hindus and Muslims, and hence the need for a separate country. Contradicting the statement here was a Muslim shrine where cows were regarded sacred. Here cows were deemed to be sacred and treated in a manner not very different from the way Hindus treat them. While we were driving we came across several cows walking on the road. Looking at them, I wondered if they were sacred, but they were not. They didn't have bags around their necks, and people incessantly honked at them to make them get out of the way. There weren't any sacred cows at the shrine either, to my disappointment.

'I am glad we didn't bring Maryam along,' I joked to

Iqbal Qaiser.

In the Hindu tradition, cow worship is associated with the cult of Krishna, who is depicted as a cowherd. However, reverence for the animal is also found in the Buddhist and Jain traditions.[89] In the Islamic tradition, one of the explanations put forth by experts for cow sacrifice is primarily to root out cow worship, which must have been a prominent cult among the Israelites as can be discerned from the cult of the worship of the golden calf at the time of Prophet Moses.[90]

'Our original shrine was in Karyana, India,' said Shadi Shah. 'It is still there, managed by Sikhs. At the time of Partition, when my grandfather migrated, he was allotted a shrine at Bhambha. The story of the cows begins from there. One of his devotees presented some cows to the saint as a present and ever since then the cows became famous as the cows of Sher Shah.'

'Are those cows still there?'

'Yes. The *malangs* there look after them.'

'I was told that there would be some cows here as well,' I said.

'There are, but they roam around. Only once during the year, on the 11th of Chaitar [month in indigenous calendar], they come to this shrine for the festival of the saint. There are about seventy to eighty cows. Earlier they used to be in thousands. But now people's religious views are changing. They no longer tolerate the cows of the saint walking through their fields. Earlier they would welcome them. It is particularly the Wahhabi-like people who have an issue with the cows.'

'While the cows roam around is there anyone who takes care of them? Do people also steal them? They are fairly expensive.'

'A few *malangs* walk around with the cows, but even if they didn't, nobody would dare to steal them because the cost for doing so is very high. Some sort of evil would befall the thief and he would have no other option but to get rid of them. Sometimes when we have to sell a cow to raise money for the festival or for renovation of the shrine, it becomes a problem because no one wants to buy them. All the butchers here know that these are the cows of the saint and slaughtering them would bring some sort of evil. Only Wahhabis buy the cows.'

Before we left, Shadi Shah agreed to show us the gurdwara. It was a triple-storey building standing on a large ground, behind which was the building where his family lived. Corrosive ash had settled over its white exterior and the floor and other structures from the inside were in a dilapidated state. However, I was pleasantly surprised to see that the plinth where once the Guru Granth Sahib must have been kept and recited was still intact and so was the original tile of the floor. The frescoes on the walls were still visible. The entrance though, was blocked with a wooden plank.

'It is for safety. The building is too unsteady now,' explained Shadi Shah. 'This gurdwara is a blessed place. Anything that I have ever wished for while praying here has been fulfilled.'

'You've been to India a few times,' said Shadi Shah, 'help me out. I want to go and visit the shrine of my ancestors at Karyana. Our devotees from there ask us to come regularly.'

'You should definitely go,' replied Iqbal Qaiser. 'The Sikhs at Karyana have maintained the shrine beautifully. It has been divided into two parts, one of which is reserved as a Muslim shrine, while the other is a gurdwara where Akhand Path is performed.'

≈

Driving at a snail's pace, we headed towards the village of Bhambha, where we had been told we would find holy cows. The distance to be covered was short, only about thirty kilometres, a matter of half an hour on a proper road, but at this speed it took much longer.

'Look at that gurdwara,' said Iqbal Qaiser, pointing to a sleek building with a small dome rising from the middle of the village of Daftu. 'That gurdwara is of immense importance. A few kilometres from here is the village of Pandoke where Bulleh Shah's father worked as an Imam in the local mosque. After his death, the chaudris of the village asked Bulleh Shah to take his place but he refused as he was uninterested. This angered the locals who planned to beat him, but before they could do so he fled from the village and headed towards Kasur. The villagers followed him and announced that anyone who gave refuge to Bulleh Shah would be beaten up. Bulleh Shah came to this gurdwara and said, "I am in the house of God. Let's see who can take me from here." The chaudris tried negotiating with the Sikhs but they refused to help, saying that they could not throw Bulleh Shah out of the house of God. Eventually after protracted discussions, Bulleh Shah was allowed to proceed to Kasur.'

We drove through the village of Bhamba asking for directions to the shrine of Bava. In the outskirts of the village, in a vacant ground on which children were playing cricket, was the shrine we were looking for. Across the road facing the shrine was the graveyard. There weren't any sacred cows here. Construction work was taking place, supervised by a *malang* wearing a red chola. The workers were junior *malangs*, who stopped working and followed us with their gaze.

'If even after becoming *malangs* they are expected to work then what is the point of even becoming one,' I joked with Iqbal Qaiser, who gave me a brief smile.

Escorted to the centre of the courtyard, we were made to sit on a mat placed on the ground, while the head *malang* sat on a chair opposite us, the dynamics of the relationship clearly established. Throughout the conversation, junior *malangs* came towards him, touched his knees to seek his blessing.

'There are two herds of cows,' said Saeen Shoukat, the senior *malang*. 'One is from Kahna and one from here. The one from this shrine is the progeny of the original herd of cows that was gifted to Saint Sher Shah whereas the herd from Kahna is bought. The cows are free to roam around. They have little bags attached to their ears in which people present their offerings. Sometimes the cows ask for the offerings themselves. They knock on doors and urge the people to present their offerings. But now the trend is decreasing. People don't believe in shrines and their traditions. Earlier people would touch the hooves of the cows for blessings. They would pass their children from under them and oil their horns. All these practices have stopped.'

'What happens when a cow dies?'

'The *malangs* give them a proper burial. For example, one of the cows died near Sahiwal, so it was buried there. Now there is a shrine there built around the grave, but I am not sure if the people there know that the shrine belongs to a cow. They think it was a saint. One of the *malangs* told me the story,' Saeen Shoukat said with a chuckle.

On the way back, we changed our route and headed towards Raiwind. I was surprised to learn that this village was so close to Sundar industrial state, and yet so underdeveloped.

'I won't be surprised if some day we find a shrine where a donkey is buried,' I said to Iqbal Qaiser.

'There is one actually,' he replied. 'It is called the shrine of Mai Mufto at a village called Toor in Lahore district. There was a donkey in the village that did not belong to anyone, and the young boys would use the animal for their personal needs, if you know what I mean. When the donkey died they decided to bury it since all of them had used it at one point or the other for free. Over the years, that grave became a shrine, and the donkey became a woman, Mai Mufto, someone who was used for free.'

'How do you know?' I asked.

'One of my friends was amongst the users of the donkey,' Iqbal Qaiser replied.

≈

On top of the ancient *pahari* sat an old man under an acacia tree. It was a fine spring day. The howling wind brought along with it a feeling of solitude. Spread across the plain, at the base of this mound, is the rapidly growing city of Shahkot. Cut off from society, one cannot help but feel spiritual here. For thousands of years, priests, Sufis, mendicants and yogis have chosen abandoned places like these to eradicate the dimension of time from their existence, to have metaphysical experiences.

From behind black frames, the old man's magnified eyes

peered through. Green and white plastic bottles filled with water stood next to him. Behind him, on the highest point of the *pahari* was the shrine of Baba Naulakh Hazari, built around a sacred rock that contained the footprints of his lion and lamb, which once stood together drinking water from the same vessel. Six hundred years ago, Baba Naulakh also would have sat here, all alone, having the ultimate spiritual experience.

I could not help but be drawn towards the old man. I had several questions for him. Nearby was a small hut made out of mud that housed photographs of the saint.

'Why are you sitting here?' I asked him.

'For Allah,' he replied.

'What do you mean?'

He said something but I didn't understand. Then he said, 'Help an old man. Give him some money in the name of Allah.'

My illusion of a higher spiritual experience was shattered. The relationship between the old man and me was reduced to that between a beggar and his benefactor. Feeling cheated I got up and walked over to the other side of the mound, away from the city and the economics it thrived on. A lush green field seemed to dance in celebration of spring. Two cranes and a few labourers were busy working on the mound, trying to flatten the land in preparation for a spacious suburban town. Acidic green water poured out of the ground as these prophets of development removed the ancient debris to make way for 'civilization'.

According to the Archaeological Report of 1994 to 1996, this *pahari* located in the outskirts of the city of Shahkot, on the Faisalabad road, dates back to the third century BCE.[91]

Walking up its mud track, we collected several pieces of ancient utensils scattered all over. On the vertical wall of the *pahari* that covered the track from one side, one could see several layers of civilization buried deep within. One of the layers was of charcoal. This showed that the city had once been burned. Pieces of human bone could be seen hidden within the earth. On top of the mound, a pyramid of ancient bricks was piled up on one side. My companions, Iqbal Qaiser and Maryam Altaf, carried one brick each on our way back from the mound. A couple of boys on a bike, heading to the shrine of Baba Naulakh Hazarai stopped and tried selling us ancient artifacts that they had collected from the mound.

'The *pahari* has been scaled down from its original size. I came here several years ago for a documentary with Pakistan television. It was much bigger then,' Iqbal Qaiser told me as we stood at the edge, lamenting the arrival of development.

'Isn't this how they discovered the ruins of Harappa? They were laying down the track for a railway when the contractor noticed ancient bricks,' I said.

This discovery had prompted Alexander Cunningham (founder and head of the Archaeological Survey of India) to immediately halt the pillage of the ruins and start excavation— and the Indus Valley Civilization took its place in ancient Indian history and became one of the oldest civilizations of the world. After Partition, archaeology was not pursued earnestly except for a brief period by the legendary Dr Ahmad Hasan Dani, who worked on the Gandharan sites in the northwest of the country. As a result, the Indus Valley Civilization continues to be the only ancient civilization of the world whose language is still to be deciphered. This is a pity given the fact that

Pakistani civilization, in one way or the other, is a continuation of that civilization.

Standing here I wondered if the key for unlocking the mystery of that language was hidden in these ruins that were being demolished by cranes. Soon there would be no *pahari* and the key, if it ever existed, would also disappear.

'They sold this land and they know that this *pahari* is being flattened to make way for a new society,' shouted the fifty-six-year-old Iqbal, a government official. He was sitting at the shrine of Baba Naulakh Hazari showing the pilgrims a glimpse of the magic rock that contained the footprints of the saint's lion and a lamb. At the arrival of devotees, who flowed in regularly, Iqbal would remove the green cloth covering with his stick. He would point to what he described to be the footprints of a lion and a lamb, and introduce the visitor to the magic qualities of the saint.

'There was no water up here. So the saint prayed to Allah and water appeared in this bowl,' he said, as he pointed to a recess within the rock. 'Both the lamb and the lion had water from here together. Now pick up one of the petals from the rock and eat it.' Reluctantly I did as I was told.

'Look at this,' he said, pointing with his stick to a collection of rocks on the side. 'This is the mark of a lamp. This mark is of the forest that was here. Look at this one. It reads Muhammad. And this one reads Allah.'

The marks that he was passing off as symbols of divinity looked ordinary to me, fossil imprints of leaves and water droplets stuck within two surfaces. Iqbal wouldn't allow his devotees to spend too much time contemplating the marks on the rock because that would lead to questions; the sort that were springing up in my mind.

'Now put some token money here on the side, for the saint,' he said.

Watching his presentation, it became clear to me why this particular brand of religion is now slowly fading away, as a more scientific and rationale interpretation of religion replaces it.

One of the criticisms against Hinduism that I have heard growing up is that Hindus worship rocks, which is why they are inferior to us. To begin with, such a reductionist statement lacks any philosophical and religious understanding of Hinduism. However, if one is to entertain this absurd idea of worshipping a rock temporarily, then the question that comes to my mind is that how is this sacred rock at a Muslim shrine any different?

Behind Iqbal was a small room made out of stones, similar to the ancient ruins of Taxila used by Buddhist monks several centuries ago.

'These are ancient structures,' said Iqbal Qaiser. 'There were several of these when I came here last time. Now all of them are gone.'

'No matter how much of the *pahari* they flatten we can be sure for now that they will not be able to raze this part because of this shrine,' he said. This was the only reason he was willing to accept an exploitative religious practice like this one.

Inside the shrine, which is located within the city, a painting on the wall depicted a lion and a lamb having water together, while next to them the name of Allah was shaped out of a rock—the sacred rock. The reference to a lion and a lamb having water together has been clearly adopted from the Biblical references of Jesus Christ returning and bringing peace to the world, of which the ultimate symbol would be the animals having water together.

'Notice how the pillar of the shrine is emerging out of a lotus flower,' said Iqbal Qaiser. The lotus has a particular significance in Hindu tradition. One of the most important Hindu deities, Lakshmi, is depicted as standing on one. The flower is also revered in Buddhism. It was interesting to see a lotus incorporated into the architecture of a Muslim shrine. It showed that despite defining Pakistani culture as being the opposite of Hindu or Indian culture, cultural symbols which have been sacred for thousands of years to the people of this region are still sacred.

On our way back from the shrine, I saw a billboard advertising the candidates for the provincial and national assemblies in this area. At the centre of the poster was a young man behind whom there was a picture of this particular shrine. He has to be from the guardian family of the shrine, I thought. Using his prestige as a member of the sacred family, he was seeking political advantage. This is another reason why shrine culture has come under attack from orthodox quarters in recent years. Cashing in on the legacy of their ancestors, the guardians of the shrine have amassed political and economic strength becoming a hegemonic power. When the orthodox attack such religious practices, they also provide a platform for the locals to challenge the control of the progeny of a saint over the region's economics and politics.

'Do you know that the story of this shrine is associated with Guru Nanak?' asked Iqbal Qaiser as we drove back to

Lahore. 'The Sikhs don't accept it but the Muslim tradition is that Guru Nanak was born by the blessing of Baba Naulakh Hazari. It is believed that Nanak's parents came to this shrine and the saint blessed them after which Nanak was born.'

## 10

## *Identity Crisis*

'GET OUT, HAROON!' shouted one of my aunts. Ignoring her, I continued photographing the women gathered in the room. Between the wrath of my aunt and that of my mother, I would rather not deal with my mother's, who had instructed me to photograph the event. My sister was to get married in a few days and tonight, all the women of the family had gathered for *millad*. Since they were all close family members and friends, I moved in and out of the room without any inhibition.

'She will only come in when you leave,' my aunt said with an increased authority.

I looked behind me to see a middle-aged woman wearing a burqa, with only her eyes visible, staring at me. Can't she even enter the room if I am here, I thought as I exited so that she could join the other ladies and give them a lesson or two on Islam, known as *dars*.

'Please no photographs,' she said to my mother.

'Don't worry. He is leaving,' she assured her.

≈

Burqa, has globally become the symbol of Muslim women. A common misconception is that all Muslim women cover themselves with it. 'I was surprised to see that hardly any women in Lahore were wearing a burqa,' noted a friend from Mumbai who was visiting Pakistan. I could relate to what she said. On my visits to India, I had noticed that the Muslims there exerted their religious identity much more than the Muslims in Pakistan. On the roads of Mumbai and Bengaluru, one came across many women wearing burqas. While wearing one has been a minority practice till now, at least in the urban centres of the country, there has been an increasing trend to 'revert' to a display of religious symbols like the beard and hijab in the past few years. I use the word revert with caution here because it implies going back to certain practices or searching for some historical roots. I believe that this is, in fact, a new phenomenon that might have parallels in Islamic history but remains a product of historical contingencies—9/11 in particular.

In a post 9/11 world, marred with religious terrorism and counter-insurgency terrorism, it seems the world is divided into two large camps—Muslims and everybody else. In these times of heightened search for identity, Muslims have turned towards their religion to grapple with the new emerging political realities. This soul searching, in many cases, has resulted in urban, educated Muslims adopting a version of Islam that is puritanical. In Pakistan, there has been an increasing trend of people being drawn towards religiosity, an Islamic tradition that is not a legacy of religious syncretism like Chistiya or Barelvi, but reactionary and exclusivist, originating out of the Deoband and Ahle-Hadith schools of thought. Given the fact that this renewed interest in Islamic identity is a product of Muslim separateness from the rest of the world, it doesn't come as a surprise that the schools of thought in vogue are those which are exclusivist.

While the impact of Islamic revivalism has trickled down to rural and 'underdeveloped' places, for the most part it remains confined to urban centres due to the existing biases of the educated class in relation to non-Muslims propagated through the Pakistani education system. In order to understand the phenomenon better, I decided to visit my former professor of Anthropology at LUMS (Lahore University of Management Sciences), Dr Sadaf Ahmad, who has recently written a book called *Transforming Faith: The Story of Al-Huda and Islamic Revivalism among Urban Pakistani Women*. Al-Huda is one of the most prominent Pakistani religious revivalist organizations, based in Islamabad, which aims to educate women about the Quran and the Sunnah. Established in 1994, in the past few years, it has spread rapidly across the educated middle class of Islamabad. Now Islamic lectures of Al-Huda are available online and are widely consumed. I was particularly interested in understanding Islamic revivalist movements in the country as a threat posed to the shrine culture discussed in this book.

Sitting across from Sadaf in her office in one of the leading universities of the country, I looked out of the window behind her and saw girls wearing jeans and freely intermingling with members of the opposite sex. The School of Social Sciences and Humanities has played a major role in protecting the secular culture of the university from the onslaught of fundamentalist Islamists. 'It [LUMS] is an interesting island,' I remember Ayesha Siddiqa, a well-known political analyst, saying once. But over the past few years, there have been rumours about the religious right slowly dominating the administration of the university and transforming its culture. Every time a liberal or a leftist professor leaves LUMS, there are rumours about the internal politics being the cause of his or her departure. The number of students at the university who have a beard or wear an abaya has increased considerably. I asked Sadaf if 'Islamic revivalist' movements like Al-Huda were also spreading into places like LUMS.

Sadaf was conscious of the fact that the display of Islamic religiosity in the university was on the rise, much like it was in general Pakistani society, but she was not sure if that could be attributed to any particular religious movement.

'I sometimes receive emails from students saying that they cannot study Anthropology of Religion. "Our faith is not strong enough at this stage," is what they say,' she told me. 'Study of Anthropology allows one to understand concepts from different perspectives. It means recognizing that different people have different truths. This, some students feel, will undermine their faith.'

I asked Sadaf if the women who were attracted to Al-Huda and were critical of shrine culture were aware of the cultural and philosophical underpinnings of these shrines.

'No,' she said. 'They criticize the rituals and rites at these shrines but beyond that they have little understanding of its culture. Most of the women who had joined Al-Huda at the time I studied them were those who had a disconnect with the local traditions. They respected the saints but were also apologetic about them. "The saints did what they did because of the conditions prevalent at that time" is a common argument they give. It is said, for example, that Muslim Sufis had to turn to qawwalis to attract Hindus who enjoyed bhajans. On the other hand, it is interesting to note that women who come from backgrounds imbued in Barelvi ethos are not easily attracted to this movement.'

'This means, according to them, there is no longer any need to practise that form of Islam because there aren't any Hindus around,' I added.

'At the classes the women are instructed about Islamic culture and ethos that is not indigenous but Arabic in essence. Local cultural practices like Basant or Mehndi are looked down upon and discouraged. Particularly, attention is given to *da'wa* [preaching of Islam] and *dars*. Women who are trained at this institution take up an active role in spreading their messages within their communities and societies through *dars*.'

'One of the main reasons behind the success of the movement is the religious background of its students. Most of the women who come to Al-Huda already have faith in Islam by virtue of growing up in a Muslim household and nation and also being educated in an Islamized education system. What they don't have is scriptural knowledge, which is then provided to them through their study of Islam at Al-Huda. Even though Al-Huda claims that it doesn't adhere to any particular school of thought, their interpretation of Islam is similar to the Ahle-Hadith strand. They thus propagate a particular understanding of Islam as "true" Islam and that is how it is perceived by its students who have no access to alternate approaches to Islamic scriptural knowledge. Another key reason why Al-Huda is successful in spreading its understanding of Islam among middle-class women is that its approach resonates with the kind of women who come to the school to study Islam. The middle class values education and as such they lean towards an institute that offers scriptural knowledge [as opposed to leaning towards a religious group which focuses on traditional rituals]. Their reason for deeming the Islamic discourse that they are exposed to as authoritative is not just related to their lack of alternative scriptural knowledge but also because they deem Farhat Hashmi, who began the school, to be a religious authority. Farhat Hashmi has a PhD in Hadith Sciences from Glasgow and heavily relies upon scientific concepts and logic to explain her religious arguments. Such credentials and such an approach resonate in a class that values education and science, and enhances the credibility of the school and subsequently its message.'

Sadaf explained that Al-Huda's proselytizing takes place in a faith-based framework that is already extant in Pakistani society through its politics and educational system. Here at the school, for the first time, these women study primary texts and understand them literally. I told her about the shrine of Baba Naulakha where the visitors who are generally uneducated are made to believe that the natural marks on the rocks are miraculous names of God and the Prophet, and thus sacred.

'For an educated mind, such a tradition would be difficult to absorb,' I commented.

'Faith or belief has little to do with education. But certainly, the fact that Al-Huda is making inroads into the elite class of the society and is able to spread a particular understanding of Islam within it, is significantly due to the fact that no other spiritual movement has been able to provide an avenue for the educated class to explore the scriptural texts in a manner that resonates with them,' Sadaf replied.

'When a puritanical religious approach becomes the dominant school of thought, could it be said then that Pakistani society would eventually become an extremist state in terms of its politics?' I asked.

'Al-Huda claims that it is an apolitical organization and strictly forbids political discussions in its classrooms. "Focus on becoming better Muslims", is what the teachers tell their students who wish to discuss political matters. They also strongly discourage participation in political rallies. So they essentially have a bottom-up approach: they train the women who Islamize the environment in their households and neighbourhoods. This eventually would create an environment in which the implementation of Sharia would be the next logical step.'

'When that happens I will grow a beard and you can wear a burqa to fit in,' I joked with her.

'That would be the time to leave the country,' she replied with a straight face.

'In this growing environment of religious puritanism, how do you think these shrines are likely to fare in the future? Would shrine culture eventually end?' I asked her.

'I don't know. I think for shrine culture to end, things would have to become much worse than they are right now, and stay that way for a considerably long period of time. This is because shrine culture is so deeply embedded in our society that it would be hard to remove it. In order to get rid of it, the next generation needs to internalize the concept that it is wrong and unIslamic. On the other hand, you can also see that there is resurgence in the interest in Sufi poetry and music. Admittedly this section of society is still a minority and for it to have any serious impact it needs to grow in size. But that is where hope lies,' Sadaf said.

≈

'Oh my God, Haroon. If you were at the session you would have killed her,' my sister told me at the end of the three-hour long *dars*. 'She said that the youth of our country have strayed away from our culture. They mimic the West or India by celebrating Valentine's Day or Basant. These festivals have nothing to do with our culture and also that women should not work because their incomes bring ill-fate to a household.'

'You don't know how I controlled myself,' Anam told me.

'I thought the session was nice,' said Uzma, my sister's friend. She has done her Master's in Journalism from a leading women's college of the country and is now a housewife. 'Some of the things she said were informative.'

'How can she even say it is unIslamic for women to work?' I asked. 'What about Hazrat Khadijah, the first wife of the Prophet? Wasn't she a businesswoman? She can only impress people who don't know history or culture. What "our" culture is she talking about? Isn't Heer Ranjha part of Punjabi culture? It is the most celebrated folk story here. For centuries it has been sung and dramatized. It is essentially a celebration of love. How is it any different from the celebration of Valentine's Day? In fact, the celebration of Heer Ranjha's love is much more profound than Valentine's Day. In our culture it has taken metaphysical dimensions, by becoming part of the folk religion. We worship love, not only celebrate it.'

≈

'Iqbal sahib, do you know that Anam is a Siyal as well? Anam do you know what is said about Siyal women in Mirza Sahiban?' I asked.

We were on our way to Jhang, the city where the legendary lovers, Heer and Ranjha, are buried in a single grave. Their shrine has now become a religious pilgrimage site and I was particularly intrigued by such treatment of love.

Using the pretext of traditions and culture on several occasions, the right to marry out of choice, the right to practise religion, etc., are curbed. I grew up with a 'modern' understanding of tradition which argued for the unshackling of society from the fetters of traditionalism to make way for progress. However, what exploring traditional and cultural history did for me was to clarify this misconception. This derogatory manner of looking at tradition is a colonial legacy that thrived on undermining the indigenous culture and exalting the British manner of living. The legend of Heer Ranjha is an example from the repository of 'tradition' that not only celebrates the love between two individuals (a pre-modern example of honouring individuality) but also raises it to metaphysical dimensions comparing the love between Heer and Ranjha to that between a believer and God.

Part of the oral tradition of South Asia, the story of Heer Ranjha has been sung by bards and dramatized by folk artists for centuries. The story was first written by a poet from Jhang called Damodar Das Arora during the reign of the Mughal Emperor Akbar. However, just the way Valmiki's Ramayana became Tulsidas's after he rewrote the epic, this legend also became Waris Shah's when he rewrote it in the eighteenth century. Today it is also referred to as Waris Shah's *Heer*.

According to Damodar's version, which was then supported by Waris Shah, *Heer Ranjha* is based on an actual story that Damodar saw unfold in front of his eyes. In the end, both Heer and Ranjha were buried in one grave, to celebrate their eternal love. Their shrine in Jhang, which, according to the legend, is the hometown of Heer, is today a popular destination where people from all over the country come to ask for blessings, especially in the matter of love. True to its pagan roots, folk religion in Pakistan has specialized shrines for particular needs—Aban Shah for fertility, the shrine of crows for people with speech impediments and Heer Ranjha for love.

When Damodar wrote the poem, it was meant to be a secular love epic. Around the same time that he lived, there was a wandering malamati Sufi in Lahore known by the name of Shah Hussain, a spectacular Punjabi poet. He for the first time, transformed the story of Heer Ranjha from a secular epic to a spiritual legend. He compared the love of Heer for Ranjha to that of a believer for his God, a theme that was subsequently picked up by Bulleh Shah and Waris Shah. Through his poetry, he introduced the concept of Wahadut-ul-Wajud, or monism, into the story which remains an essential part of Hindu philosophy and Islamic spirituality.

'Mahi mahi kook di mein ape Ranjhan hoyi
Ranjhan Ranjhan sab koi akho, Heer na akhon koi'
(Calling the name of my beloved I myself have become Ranjhan
Call me Ranjhan only now as I am no longer Heer)

'Do you know what Peelu, the writer of Mirza Sahiban

[another famous folk love legend of Punjab] says about Siyal women, Anam?' Iqbal Qaiser asked her. She did not. Turning around to face her, he recited:

> 'Evil are the dealings of the Siyals; evil the way to the Siyals;
> Evil the women of the Siyals; be not bewitched by them.
> They will take out thy liver and eat it; lay not this trouble upon me.'[92]

'But why does everyone hate Siyal women?' she asked.

'This is Mirza's mother warning Mirza not to chase the love of Sahiban. At this part of the story, Sahiban is about to marry her cousin and Mirza, having heard the news, is planning to elope with her. Citing the example of Heer, Mirza's mother is trying to dissuade her,' Iqbal Qaiser clarified.

'So then this is the view of Sahiban's mother-in-law,' Anam said, glancing suggestively at me through the rear-view mirror.

'Yes,' said Iqbal Qaiser.

We exited from the junction of Pindi Bhattiyan on the motorway and headed towards Chiniot which was en route to Jhang. '*Naukar Sahaba da* [I am the servant of the companions],' read a graffiti on a board announcing that we were heading towards the hotbed of sectarian conflict in Punjab—Jhang. The militant organization, Lashkar-e-Jhangvi, blamed for the recent massacre of Shias, originated in Jhang which still serves as the movement's capital. One bone of contention between the Shia and Sunni sects is the status of the companions of the Prophet, especially the first three—Abu Bakr, Umar and Usman. The Shias maintain that they were usurpers of power which should have actually been given to the cousin and son-in-law of the Prophet, Ali. The Sunnis, on the other hand, argue that a democratic process was followed after the demise of the Prophet and Abu Bakr, who became the next leader of the Muslim community, followed by Umar and Usman, was a rightly guided pious Caliph. 'I am the servant of the companions', was a political statement by Sunni extremists. Behind the board, black flags with 'alms', the symbol of the Shia community, emerged at the top of the shops and houses. This was contested territory.

'Let's stop here for a little while,' suggested Iqbal Qaiser looking at a board that read Tiba Shah Behlol. 'A short distance from here is the shrine of Behlol under a grove of banyan trees. He was the spiritual master of Shah Hussain.'

It was a fantastic sight—about five to six ancient banyan trees with their drooping boughs, in quick succession. I could imagine Hindu yogis wearing saffron-coloured clothes, intermingling with sadhus smeared with ash, sitting next to Sufi malamatis under these trees. Here they must have exchanged ideas about religion, philosophy, rites and God that now transcend the nationalistic boundaries that have been created after Partition. Somewhere in these trees, in this land and in the air, those conversations are still preserved and can be heard in the silence of civilization, in the rustling of leaves, in the howling of the wind. They would remain here for eternity.

In a small building behind the trees, I met a few women visiting from the city of Chiniot.

'We have come to perform Nauratre. This is for a special wish,' the oldest among them told me.

'Can you tell me what the wish is?' I asked.

An uncomfortable silence followed. The woman stared at me, judging me because I did not know the decorum to be followed for special wishes. One is never supposed to tell one's wish.

'What do you do for Nauratre?' I asked.

'We stay up for nine nights praying to the saint to grant our wishes,' the woman replied.

This is a Muslim version of the Hindu festival Navratri for which devotees stay up for nine consecutive nights praying to the goddess Durga. The goddess is replaced by a saint here.

'Are you Shia?' I asked her.

'Yes.'

'What is your name?'

Once again she stared at me blankly. She was judging me again because I did not know that it was inappropriate to ask Shias to identify themselves at a time like this and at a place like this.

≈

Our stop at Chiniot was going to be short; we planned to rush through the unfortunate haveli of Omar Hayat. Completed in 1935 this was a fine example of woodwork for which Chiniot has been popular. To the residents of the haveli though this was a cursed house that first claimed the life of the father and then the son, followed by his mother. The mother and the son are buried in the main hall. After Partition, the structure fell into disrepair resulting in its top two floors crashing down. A few years ago, the haveli was taken over by the government of Pakistan and then renovated to serve as a museum and a library.

More than the architectural splendour of the building,

I was interested in the conversation that was taking place between two government employees sitting in the main hall, both of them sporting beards, a sign of religiosity.

'In Burma when the Christians were massacring Muslims, they were killing 20,000 people every day,' said one of them. I was tempted to clarify that it was Buddhists and not Christians who were involved in this religious violence, but then I saw no point in directing the official's hatred from Christians towards Buddhists.

'Are all the insults only reserved for Muslims? Why should we tolerate this? Why? The mob did absolutely the right thing by burning down the houses of those blasphemous Christians,' the official continued.

Just a couple of days prior to our visit to Chiniot, an angry mob of Muslims in Lahore had burned down 170 Christian houses. The rage had been ignited by an argument between two friends, a Christian and a Muslim, while they were enjoying their evening drinks. Ironically, before the angry mob burned down the Christian colony to protect the honour of their Prophet, the 'blasphemous' Christian was already in police custody.

'But this is not the teaching of the Prophet,' argued the other official. 'To shed the blood of a single human being is like killing the entire humanity, the Prophet has said.' His companion was fuming with rage and retorted in an angry tone. However, the other man was also not one to give up easily. He continued arguing citing from the Quran and the Hadith in vain. I wanted to walk up to him and tell him to stop arguing by putting my hand on his shoulder. I wanted to caution him that reports about blasphemy are borne out of heated discussions like these, of which Muslims have also been victims like non-Muslims. But I didn't.

≈

'You mean Sahiban's mosque,' replied a vendor when Iqbal Qaiser asked him about the old mosque of the village. We were in Kheiwa, the historic village brought to 'disrepute' by its rebellious daughter Sahiban.

On Mirza's arrival, Sahiban, instead of getting married to her cousin, eloped with Mirza. Sahiban's brothers had chased them and eventually were able to kill the lovers. In revenge, Mirza's brothers had raided this village and burned it down. Only one structure had survived, the mosque where Mirza and Sahiban fell in love while studying the Quran together as children.

Every girl and woman we saw here was a Sahiban. She was bold, proactive, eager to engage in a conversation with us. I have found that women in villages tend to be less inhibited than their urban counterparts, but this characteristic seemed more pronounced in this village.

'Have you come here to see Sahiban's mosque?' a group of women asked us, as we balanced precariously on a thin path dividing various fields. Some of the younger ones laughed at our jugglery.

I wondered what Sahiban meant to them. I wanted to ask them, but we were in a rush. Sahiban in folk culture is depicted as a disloyal lover who had betrayed Mirza for the love of her brothers. When her brothers were near them, she hid Mirza's bows and arrows in a tree, as she knew that he would be able to kill them easily. As a result, her brothers could kill Mirza. Mirza had died feeling betrayed. Recent scholars, however, have argued that the depiction of Sahiban has been too harsh. She had been like a modern woman, torn between her loyalty for her family and her lover. In this way she was different from Heer, who had been clear that she only wanted Ranjha and was willing to sacrifice her family for him. Sahiban had understood the complexities of life, while Heer's perspective had been more black and white. So whereas Heer's love for Ranjha has been glorified and raised to metaphysical dimensions, the love affair of Mirza Sahiban is ridiculed, believed to be an example of a love dominated by carnal desire unlike the spiritual love story of Heer Ranjha. In fact the story of Mirza Sahiban is such a blemish on the legacy of spiritual love stories of Punjab, that it was said that these two brought an end to the era of love legends by their ignominious love affair. It is commonly said:

'*Sahiban kaach zamane di* (Sahiban belongs to an era of moral decline)
*Te Mirza suur da lun*' (whereas Mirza is the penis of a swine)

≈

An intimidating group of jeeps rushed past us almost throwing us off the single-lane road. Their windows were blackened, and black uniformed guards sat in the rear touting their machine guns. We assumed them to be either members of the Sipah-e-Sahaba, now known as Ahle Sunnat Wal Jamaat or Laskhar-e-Jhangvi, both Sunni hardline organizations that fuel the sectarian conflicts in the country. After Sipah-e-Sahaba was banned by President Pervez Musharraf in 2002, it re-emerged with its new name of Ahle Sunnat Wal Jamaat and continues playing an active role in the politics of the country. Since elections were only a few months away, billboards with photographs of its leader, Muhammad Ahmed Ludhianvi, decorated the length and breadth of the city.

Ever since the rise in target killings of prominent Shias in the major cities of the country, human rights activists, opposition party leaders and segments of the media have alleged that the Punjab government, dominated by the right-winged Pakistan Muslim League Noon, has been supporting these radical outfits who are based in Jhang. It is said that the right-winged party is eager to maintain ties with these extremist organizations because of their control over the electorate. The Muslim League Noon, on the other hand, rubbishes the claims. However, going by the omnipresence of the Ahle Sunnat Wal Jamaat all over the city, it was clear that there was some truth behind the accusations.

Ludhianvi as a suffix reveals that his origin is from the Indian city of Ludhiana. His family must have migrated at the time of Partition. The trauma of being uprooted from his ancestral city must have stayed with young Muhammad Ahmed. The fact that he continues to use Ludhianvi with his name highlights the emotional bond that he has with the city which is no longer his. I wondered how much of a role the riots of Partition and displacement from his home played on the psyche of Muhammad Ahmed. By turning to religious extremism, was he giving vent to his frustration? Was there a connection between the haphazard partition of India and the sectarian conflict in Pakistan? Would Muhammad Ahmed

Ludhianvi have been an extremist politician had the partition of India never occurred?

'The shrine of Mai Heer', noted a board on the road. 'What is Mai?' I asked Iqbal Qaiser.

'It is used out of respect. Baba is for males and Mai for females,' he explained.

The shrine was located at the top of an ancient mound, surrounded by a plethora of graves. A small market had burst into life here. Ignoring the calls of vendors selling threads, bangles and lockets, we climbed the stairs towards the shrine. In the courtyard, sitting under a *waan* tree, a lone musician sang Shah Hussain (Punjabi Verses) on his harmonium.

'O Mother, to whom should I now narrate these tales of my pains?' he sang.

Walking into the main shrine, I wondered if Heer was a Shia or a Sunni. Did it even matter?

Amanullah, the caretaker of the shrine, greeted the devotees telling them about the miracles of this place.

'Girls looking to get married, tie bangles here. Young couples who want to get married but cannot for some reason, tie threads here and their problem is alleviated. Barren women present cradles here and with the blessings of Mai Heer they are gifted a child.'

The cradle offering has uncanny similarities to the cult of Lord Krishna.

'Do people also sing Heer here?' I asked him.

'Let them try doing that and they will not be able to recognize themselves after a few minutes,' he retorted in repressed anger. 'We don't allow that here. These poets and bards do not understand the spiritual essence of the legend of

Heer Ranjha. This was not a love between two individuals but a spiritual love. It was pure. The poets and singers present it as a worldly story. The Siyals of the city have strictly forbidden anyone from singing or reciting Heer here.'

'Is the shrine under the control of the Siyals?' I asked him.

'Yes, it is. When the Pakistani movie *Heer Ranjha* was released in the seventies, it was played in all the cinemas of the country, except for Jhang. When one of the cinemas in Jhang tried playing it, it was burned down to the ground.'

This was a strangely comical situation. On the one hand, the Siyals, who were still in control of the shrine, were reaping benefits from the tradition of Heer Ranjha. On the other hand, there was an attempt to downplay the cultural traditions that had developed around Heer. Several centuries later, the 'honour' of their 'daughter' was still haunting the Siyal community here. *Heer* cannot be sung or played here because it presented their 'daughter' as a rebellious girl who had eloped with Ranjha even after her marriage, therefore bringing disrepute to the Siyal family, something that the Siyals are not willing to forget even today. What was comical was that while they objected to the romanticizing of the folk love legend because of honour issues, they were cashing in on the same love legend by keeping all the monetary offerings presented to the shrine. The Siyals had no qualms when it came to extracting benefit from their 'daughter'.

Amanullah was also a Siyal, a proud one. I wondered if he knew that the poem of Shah Hussain being sung outside also had a reference to the love legend:

'I roamed all around searching for my Ranjhan
Little that I knew my Ranjhan was always with me'

The walls of the shrine were filled with love messages written by pen: 'You may never be mine but I wish that wherever you live you may spend a happy life. Murad. Xox.' 'Zainab and Imran forever.' 'Salute to the love legend Mai Heer and Baba Ranjha.'

In a hotbed of religious violence, these were fascinating messages of love in honour of Heer and Ranjha.

'Do you know in a lot of villages, the recitation of Waris Shah's *Heer* is not allowed. People believe that if the sounds of the verses fall on the ears of young girls, they too will elope like Heer,' Iqbal Qaiser told us.

≈

It was dark already and the city of Chistian was still a few kilometres away. Historically, Sufi shrines remained open throughout the night, giving refuge to supplicants arriving at any time of the day. But ever since these shrines have become a target for Islamic militants, devotees, at least at the major shrines, were asked to exit by a fixed time and the shrine is shut for the night. For this particular shrine, we had travelled to southern Punjab, believed to be the hub of shrine culture in the country. The city of Chistian is a few kilometres away from the important city of Bahawal Nagar.

We crossed over the railway track and headed in the direction of what is locally referred to as old Chistian. Darkness engulfed us as we drove on this lonely road. Out of the abyss shone the colourful lights decorating the shrine. A police official deployed at the entrance stood up to greet us when we reached the shrine, but we ignored him and entered the courtyard.

'Let's visit the other shrine before it shuts,' said Iqbal Qaiser, taking us into an alley, away from the dome of the main shrine. Next to a graveyard stood a small building adorned in pink marble inside and outside.

In dismay Iqbal Qaiser said, 'It has stopped. This is where it used to happen.'

He stroked the marble.

'Young lovers who had certain impediments in their relationships would write their names on these walls with the oil of lamps from the neighbouring graves, with the belief that all their worries would be cured.'

In our eagerness to photograph the shrine and its rituals, we had failed to notice a small segment on the external wall devoid of the fancy tile work. There was a heart cut out of tile up on the wall and under it names of young lovers were clumsily written in black. This was shown to us by a man who was cleaning a grave next to the shrine. He brought us a used lamp from one of the graves with which Anam and I wrote our names on the wall.

'Please tell us about this tradition and be honest,' said Iqbal Qaiser to our guide.

'What can I say? People have their own beliefs. If someone feels that their wishes come true here then who am I to say no to them,' he replied. He was carefully avoiding the question, perhaps out of propriety. It is no longer socially acceptable to talk about love outside of wedlock. How this tradition emerged remained unanswered.

'This is the grave of the nephew of Hazrat Tajuddin Chisti, the grandson of Baba Farid Shakarganj of Pakpattan. That is the shrine of Hazrat Tajuddin Chisti,' he said pointing towards the dome decorated with colourful lights.

According to *Tajul Auliya*, a book written by a resident of this city, Chistian was founded by the grandson of Hazrat Baba Farid Shakarganj. The author notes that there used to be an old fort here outside of which was a jungle. Within that jungle there was a spot where Baba Farid had spent some time in meditation. Later when the saint settled at Pakpattan, he asked his grandson, Tajuddin Chisti to populate the place of his meditation, so the saint had come and settled here establishing this city. The name of the city is derived from the syncretistic school of thought that Baba Farid and his progeny espoused to.[93]

'Do you know this is the largest graveyard in Asia,' said our guide. I leaped over the boundary wall of the complex to see the plain marked by graves stretching until the dark horizon of the night. On the way back to the new Chistian, I realized that the boundless darkness on both sides was that of death. We were driving through a huge graveyard, an entire city of graves.

# 11

# The Changing Landscape

SCRAMBLING FOR PAPER to burn for cooking, the young girl found some discarded in one corner of her impoverished surroundings. Before putting them in her bag, she tried to decipher the words written on them but couldn't. She was illiterate.

Later at night, when an angry mob gathered around her house, screaming for her blood, the girl wondered what wrong she had done. The police arrived and arrested the fourteen-year-old. A case of blasphemy was lodged against her for burning the pages of the Quran. The fact that the girl was illiterate or suffered from Down Syndrome was not taken into account.

This is the story of Rimsha Masih, a Christian girl living in a small settlement within the capital city of Pakistan. The facts of the case are contested. Later evidence showed that the burned pages were planted by the Muslim prayer leader of the local mosque to boost up this false case. The Supreme Court of Pakistan eventually released the girl and lodged a case against the prayer leader.

Fearing for their lives after the arrest of the young girl, the Christian families of the area, numbering around 200, abandoned their houses and camped some distance away. The recent history of Pakistan shows that alleged cases of blasphemy are not settled only by the arrest of the accused, but by attacks on the immediate family, even the entire community, if the accused is a member of a religious minority.

That fateful night of August when Rimsha Masih was arrested, marks a low point in the recent religious and political history of the country. A crazed mob, eager to protect the sanctity of their religion, was willing to rip apart the young girl. A new standard of religious extremism had been set by this act; a standard that one can only hope is never met again. The act reflects how dangerous the combination of religion and politics is in Pakistan, and the lethal consequences it is likely to have.

Understanding the actions of the crazed mob in the light of history, one can decipher that there is now a fundamental difference in how people interpret religion. Jürgen Wasim observes that historically, Muslim societies have looked at 'fools and the mentally disturbed as God's favorites. The madmen and "wise fools" (*'uqala' al-majanin*) are considered exempted from canon law by God Himself; they enjoy the free rein of the religiously confused.'[94] He further states, 'In South Asia, people treat the truly mentally disturbed with remarkable patience and indulgence since their symptoms are often understood as manifestations of the Divine.'[95]

On seeing how Muslim fanatics went for the blood of a young helpless girl on the other hand, one can see that reinterpretation of religion has brought religious fundamentalism and extremism into the social fabric of Pakistan.

≈

We were heading to southern Punjab, to a small village called Tibba Haji Deen, to visit a shrine reserved for the mentally challenged. I had heard that those who suffer from mental illness are brought and left at the shrine for a few days, and they become normal again. The village was about five hours by road from Lahore and we broke our monotonous journey by taking short breaks. One of the places we stopped at was Shergarh, about an hour from Lahore, where we witnessed the festivities at the annual festival of Daud Bandagi Kirmani.

≈

Halting at the threshold of the shrine, he said a silent prayer. He touched the base of the entrance and entered. Just before entering he glanced at me. His eyes were smeared in kohl, there was a vertical mark on his forehead and he wore a glass earring on his right ear. It was an intense look. His thin black clothes revealed the colour of his skin and there was a thick bangle on his right ankle.

'They only drape a shawl when they are in public,' Iqbal Qaiser whispered into my ear, as if making sure the *malang* couldn't hear us. We were standing at a reasonable distance from him but were captivated by his aura. 'When they are with other *malangs* they wear nothing but a small lungi.'

The *malang* had shaved his head and didn't have any facial hair.

'They are Nanghe sadhus, aren't they?' I asked.

Circling around the grave of the saint Daud Bandagi, the *malang* stopped at a spot where he kissed the footprints of the saint engraved on a small marble platform.

'If you go to Jain temples there are footmarks of their prominent priests which become objects of veneration. This is exactly like that,' Iqbal Qaiser pointed out.

'This *malang* looks like a Digamabar Jain monk who remove all their body hair and roam around naked,' I observed, to which Iqbal Qaiser nodded in agreement.

'There has to be some sort of an inspiration from that particular Jain sect as well,' he said.

According to the *Encyclopaedia of Sikh Literature*, the sect called Nanghe Sadhu derives its origin from the eldest son of Guru Nanak, Shri Chand. Shri Chand had a student called Baba Gurdita who trained four disciples: Balu Hasna, Al Mast, Phool Shah and Govinda, who later formed four different sects. Some people believe that the first two disciples, Balu Hasna and Al Mast, were Muslims, while others deny this claim. Even though these sects didn't fall under the purview of mainstream Sikhism, they continued receiving the patronage of the Sikh gurus. Initially these sadhus dressed up like Sikhs by wearing a turban to cover their long hair and saffron-coloured clothes similar to Baba Nanak. They wore a black scarf around their necks and sang hymns on their tomba.

Gradually however, as Sikhism headed towards greater institutionalization, the Nanghe Sadhu started expressing their separate identity through their coiffure. Some grew their hair and let it hang on their shoulders, while others like the Digamabar Jain monks, removed all their body hair.

222 ≈ In Search of Shiva

They took off their clothes and wore nothing but lungis. This is when they came to be known as Nanghe Sadhu or the naked sadhus. Adopting severer ascetic traditions, they began scrubbing oil and ash on their naked bodies in a symbolic gesture that expressed hatred for everything worldly. Ash in the Hindu tradition represents cremation, and hence death. They isolated themselves from mainstream society and ended up living in their secluded communities known as *deras*. In an act of defiance, they refused to acknowledge the supremacy of the Guru Granth Sahib as the eternal guru and instead started worshipping the book written by Guru Gobind Singh known as the Dasant Granth.

It is believed that Muslims were attracted to this movement due to Balu Hasna and Al Mast. However, instead of reciting the Dasant Granth, they stuck to the Quran and the teachings of the Sufis. Apart from the scriptures, all the other practices like remaining secluded without clothes, and rubbing ash and oil remained. They chant hymns of Al Mast for spiritual purposes. In the Pakistani context, their devotion is centred on the shrine of the malamati saint, Shahbaz Qalandar. However, they spend their lifetime travelling from one shrine to the next, following *urs* celebrations. This has also earned them the name of Udasi Sadhu. *Udasi* in Sanskrit means pilgrimage. The Udasi Sadhus spend their entire life in pilgrimage.

Driving out of Shergarh towards Tibba Haji Deen, we drove past a small group of ascetics walking barefoot on the road. The eldest of them wore a black shawl that partially covered his torso and loin. There was a green turban on his head, while a belt of bells hung around his waist. Maryam and Iqbal Qaiser got out of the car to photograph the ascetics who, ignoring the clicking of the cameras, continued walking, oblivious to the rest of the world. Did these *malangs* know that in their asceticism they were Shiva, the ascetic?

≈

When Muhammad bin Qasim, the first Muslim conqueror of India, took over Multan, its subsidiary Chunian also fell under his control. Chunian's ruler was a Hindu whose caste was Cambho. Being the victor, Muhammad bin Qasim demanded that the ruler now pay him war indemnity, in other words money to have colonized them. This was a large sum which the ruler could not pay immediately, so he asked for some time and as collateral agreed to present his son, Maha Chawar, to the teenage Arab invader.

Soon after, the Umayyad Caliph in Damascus called back the young general and Maha Chawar travelled with him. Five years later when the Hindu ruler of Chunian was able to pay the war compensation and earned back his prince, he learned that his son, living under the influence of Muslims in Arabia, had become a Muslim. Instead of being given a warm welcome he was seen as a renegade and an 'untouchable'. The Hindu priests with considerable influence in the court of the king warned him that his son was no longer one of theirs and should either be sent back to the Muslims or killed. Sending him back to Arabia was seen as a difficult task so it was agreed that he would be killed.

Maha Chawar had a sister by the name of Kangna, who overheard the nefarious plan of her father's priest ministers. Taking her brother along she fled the city but the forces of her father soon caught up with them, and killed them near the city of Mandi Borewala. Years later, a mausoleum was constructed for the fallen prince and his sister, to commemorate the memory of one of the earliest Muslim martyrs in South Asia. According to *Tarekh-e-Cambho,* a book written by a resident of Chunian, the shrine of Diwan Chawali Mushahiq Haji Muhammad Sheikh at the village of Tibba Haji Deen was raised on the spot where Maha Chawar and his sister had been killed.

When we visited the shrine, we were asked to sit in a special room reserved for guests of the shrine's *gadi nasheen.* Outside the verandah, on a vacant ground, his car glimmered and his number plate read, 'Gadi Nasheen Tibba Haji Deen'. He sat opposite us, in a crisp shalwar kameez, occasionally playing with his gold watch. His Gucci shoes shone under the beams of sunlight that entered the room. There was an air of pompous authority around him, of a life spent being looked after.

'Last year ninety lakh rupees were collected on the occasion of the annual festival of the saint,' he said. 'This is not taking into account all the silver and gold that was offered. But the Auqaf Department refuses to spend any money on the renovation of the shrine. Please do something about it. Write in the newspapers so that our pleas are also brought in front of the world.'

What the caretaker did not mention was that he was getting his share of the sum as stipend for being the *gadi nasheen* of the saint. And this is not taking into account all the gifts they are offered for their special blessings and prayers.

'So how did your family become the guardian of this shrine?' Iqbal Qaiser asked him bluntly. 'Because in the history books there is no mention of Maha Chawar's children.' I was surprised by his audacity and beginning to wonder when they would throw us out.

'I don't know. We have never really taken an interest in our family history. Perhaps if my father was alive he would have been able to give you some information,' he replied rather sheepishly.

'You have made millions out of this shrine, the least you can do is take some interest in its history,' I felt like saying but instead took a sip of the drink that had been offered to us out of hospitality.

'Do you know that the saint was converted by Imam Hassan [the grandson of the Prophet of Islam] himself?' his brother said trying to change the topic. Of course this wasn't true. But it did imply that the shrine was very old, going all the way back to the early days of Islam. 'He, along with his sister, was martyred here,' he added.

'By whom?' I asked.

'Infidels,' he replied.

'Why?'

I received a blank expression in response. Why would the infidels need an excuse to kill Muslims?

'So why is this shrine associated with the mentally disturbed?' I asked realizing that it was time to ask questions our hosts could answer with some ease.

'It's a blessing of the saint. Those who are mentally disturbed are brought here by their families and left here for some time. Fetters are put around their ankles and enclosed with a lock. Then after about three, four, five or nine days, the lock opens by itself and the person is cured. We then ask the family members to take back the person,' he explained.

'Is everyone cured?'

'Yes, everyone.'

We walked towards the shrine and I noticed people roaming around with shackles on their feet.

'Look here. He is mental. Come here, you! Show your chain,' ordered the guardian to a confused man trying to join the group that was following us. He lifted his shalwar and we saw a small chain with a lock. It seemed to be symbolic in nature and did not hinder movement.

'This is another mental,' shouted an excited child dragging a young man twice his size with his arm.

'No, I am not mental. I have come to see the shrine,' protested the young man. I noticed a small chain around his ankle as well.

'Listen, stop asking to see more. This is inhumane,' Anam told me in English trying to conceal her frustration.

'No they are not mental,' said the guardian, monitoring the progress of the conversion. 'Don't call them mental,' he said to the children. 'Those who are violent are tied to trees or tied in the verandah.'

We walked out of the shrine towards the space where these 'dangerous' patients were chained. A teenage boy tied to the gate at the entrance excitedly waved towards his imaginary friend at the rear of this courtyard.

'There are girls,' he whispered. 'Photograph this car,' he said to Maryam who looked at me in a confused expression. 'Do you want to photograph it from the inside?'

'I am done, thank you,' she replied.

'Take one from the front then,' he insisted.

'Please listen to my complaints as well,' said a man as we were on our way out of the shrine and the guardian was no longer with us. 'I have been here for the past ten years. I am stuck here. My family will not take me back. They don't want me to get healthy. They perform black magic on me. I cannot concentrate on anything because of their evil spells.'

'But why would your family cast a black magic spell on you?' I asked him.

'So that I don't succeed in anything I do. My head hurts all the time. Please write about me. My name is Muhammad Zafar, I am thirty-five years old, from village Padoke, district Khanewal.'

We walked around the outer boundary of the shrine heading towards 'the well of Baba Farid', the famous Muslim mystic from the twelfth century. According to tradition, he hung himself inside a well not far from the shrine, while performing religious meditation for a number of days. Signs on the walls pointed towards the well. There were several pilgrims here, walking barefoot on the dusty roads of the village, out of respect for the holy village.

The well was covered by an iron cage, on which devotees had tied saffron-coloured threads. Standing next to me, a boy pulled up some water from the well and put it in vessels for the pilgrims to consume.

'Drinking water from this well will cure all your problems!' shouted a shrine official.

There were coins and notes at the base of the well, thrown in by pilgrims to seek the blessings of the saint.

'Baba Farid did not hang inside the well, as it is believed,' said the official after he took us to a separate room. 'This well belonged to his family. Baba Farid was born here and this well was part of his house.'

'Wasn't he born in Kothewal?' Iqbal Qaiser asked.

'This is Kothewal. Kothewal was its old name,' he told us.

Next to the well of Baba Farid was an abandoned gurdwara, associated with Baba Guru Nanak. 'The last time I came here, this was in a horrible condition. After my book a lot of voices were raised to protect the sanctity of the shrine. Several letters were written to Prime Minister Yousuf Raza Gilani who finally heeded to the demand and ordered the renovation of the shrine,' said Iqbal Qaiser.

Now its walls were neatly plastered and painted mango-yellow. There were several families living here when Iqbal Qaiser had visited several years ago. All of them had been evicted and only one had been allowed to stay to take care of the shrine. A plaque on the newly renovated gurdwara stated that the renovation work had been completed in 2008. Inside the main chamber was a portrait of Guru Nanak.

'Several people have come to live here but the spirit of Guru Nanak doesn't let them. He beats them up with a stick at night so they leave in the morning,' said an old man who was living here.

'I can't imagine Nanak beating up poor souls with a stick,' I said to Iqbal Qaiser who laughed politely. 'Do you think it is possible that Nanak came here to explore the heritage of Baba Farid? We know that he was fascinated by Baba Farid's poetry which was later also recorded in the Guru Granth Sahib. By visiting the city of Farid's birth, Nanak probably wanted to pay homage to the Muslim saint,' I said.

We walked across the village to the house where Baba

Farid was born. In an open courtyard were seven graves. An old man, responsible for looking after the shrine, told us that the graves belonged to Baba Farid's father, grandfather, uncles, and siblings. In a corner, he pointed out a small grave which he said belonged to one of his ancestors who, like him, also spent her life looking after this sacred place.

'Our family has been serving this shrine for the past seven generations,' he told me.

I wondered if his family once served the family of the Muslim saint before they moved to Pakpattan. I wondered if seven generations was rhetorical, to emphasize that they have been here for a long period of time.

'I am soon going to put up Baba Farid's family tree here. I have given it for composing,' he said.

Irrespective of whether his family ever served the family of the Sufi saint, I was excited to see the tradition of passing oral history from generation to generation, being practised here. This man was not educated but he knew the saint's poetry and his family history. He hadn't read this anywhere but had learned it from his elders, who had learned it from their elders. It was truly remarkable.

'The shrine we saw earlier was very disturbing,' Anam said on the drive out of the village. She had been taken a few Psychology courses at university and has particular interest in the subject. 'But this is not much different from how they treat patients at mental hospitals. Their cells are like cages there,' she added.

We spent the night at Bahawal Nagar and the next morning had breakfast with my father's old school friend Arshaad.

'This is Raju,' my father's friend said, holding a skinny

man by his shoulders. 'You went to his mohalla last year.'

He was referring to my earlier visit to Bahawal Nagar to document a Hindu festival.

'So you live at Akaliyan mohalla?' I asked Raju.

'No. I live near the civil hospital,' he replied.

'But he is a Hindu,' Arshaad explained.

Raju and I nodded at each other.

'Last year Raju took his nephew to the shrine of Haji Deen. Raju tell them the story,' my father's friend urged.

'My nephew, who is about fifteen-sixteen years old, was disturbed. He would get angry over minor issues and would disappear from the house for days. So we took him to the shrine and the guardian there told us to leave him there for four days. Four days later when we returned he was cured. Now he works at the hospital,' Raju said.

As we headed back to Lahore after breakfast, Anam commented on the story of Raju's nephew and said, 'Poor child. What trauma he must have gone through. What he was suffering from was teenage angst. Who hasn't thrown a few tantrums at that age? Imagine being chained for that.'

# Acknowledgments

This book would not have seen the light of the day without the help and support of a few people. First and foremost I am obliged to my wonderful wife, Anam Zakaria. She brings stability to my life and without her constant support I would have not been able to follow my passion.

I am also thankful to Iqbal Qaiser, my guru and mentor. I would not have managed to complete this research without his guidance and I hope that one day I would be able to help a young researcher like he helped me.

My father has been a constant source of inspiration to me. It is from him that I have inherited the love of reading and writing. My enthusiasm for travel developed by listening to stories of his journeys.

I would also like to thank my agent Kanishka Gupta, for having faith in me and my work when no one else was willing to take the risk. I am grateful to my editor at Rupa Publications, Jyotsna Mehta, who worked patiently with me. I believe the editor of the book is the unsung hero.

Finally I would like to thank my friends and colleagues,

who share with me an interest in exploring my country's history and heritage through travel. They not only willingly travelled with me but also shared the cost so that this project could see the light of the day. Thank you Maryam Altaf, Bilal Ejaz and Rida Arif!

# Notes

1.  Pruthi, *Indus Civilization*, 64.
2.  Ibid.
3.  Vedas are the oldest Hindu scriptures believed by to be written over several centuries starting from 1000 BCE.
4.  Chakravarti, *The Concept of Rudra Siva Through the Ages*, 108.
5.  Ibid., 110.
6.  Ibid., 107.
7.  In the Islamic tradition people with psychological complexities are regarded to be closer to God compared to ordinary people because of their lack of interest in the material world.
8.  Senior archaeologists like Mark Kenoyer have rubbished the Aryan invasion theory. For more detail on this please refer to the book, *The Indo-Aryan Controversy*.
9.  Frembgen, *Journey to God*.
10. Ibid., 115-116.
11. Fair, *The Madrassah Challenge*, 58.
12. Kamran, *The Evolution of Deobandi Islam in the Punjab*.
13. Baxter, *Pakistan on the Brink*, 180.
14. A voluntary, non-compulsory prayer offered by Muslims in the night to show one's devotion to God.

15. *Lun* is penis. *Lun* is a common Punjabi slang used to say that you have given me nothing or there is nothing that you have which I could use.

16. It would be illegal to call it a mosque according to the Constitution of Pakistan. In some countries including India Ahmadis are considered to be a sect within Islam, but in Pakistan the law declares them to be non-Muslims therefore they are a religious minority.

17. Fire. A place where a saint spends some time is referred to his or her *dhoan*, which they used to light there during the duration of their stay.

18. James, *The Tree of Life*, 24.

19. Ibid.

20. Sleeman, *Rambles and Recollections of an Indian Official*, 169.

21. Here I am using the translation used by Miranda Shaw in her book, *Buddhist Goddess of India*.

22. Shaw, *Buddhist Goddess of India*, 328.

23. Anonymous, *Cultus Arborum*, 61.

24. Gupta, *Encyclopedia of India, Pakistan and Bangladesh*, 1728.

25. Elgood, *Hinduism and Religious Art*, 194.

26. Joshi and Patel, *Glimpses of Indian Culture*, 15.

27. Jaffrelot, *A History of Pakistan and its Origin*, 226.

28. Ibid.

29. Thursby, *Hindu-Muslim Relations in British India*, 136.

30. Rana, *Terrifying Muslims*, pp. 129 and 130.

31. Thursby, *Hindu-Muslim Relations in British India*, 136.

32. Dalrymple, *City of Djinns*, 17-2.

33. Frembgen, *Journey to God*, 101.

34. Kishore, *Lord Shiva*, 28.

35. Ibid.

36. Frembgen, *Journey to God*, 173.
37. Ibid.
38. Ibid., 173-4.
39. Ibid., 72.
40. Ibid., 100.
41. Frembgen, *Journey to God*, 99, 100, 101.
42. Kamran, *The Evolution of the Deobandi School of Thought*.
43. Ibid.
44. On 4 January 2011 the Governor of Punjab Salman Taseer was shot down by one of his bodyguards, Mumtaz Qadri, for supporting the cause of a Christian woman, Aasia Bibi, accused of blasphemy. Following the assassination, Mumtaz Qadri became an instant hero, and was hailed by the lawyers' community. The retired chief justice of the Lahore High Court, Khwaja Sharif, offered to fight his case free of charge calling him a hero of Islam.
45. Jürgen Wasim Frembgen in his book, *Journey to God*, explaining the concept of Sufi saint as medical healers writes: 'One of the essential manifestation of popular Muslim piety is the veneration of saints. Saints act as intercessors and mediators between man and the Almighty and transcendent Allah. Within this bestowing type of religion they are like bridgeheads to the Divine. Due to their proximity to God, they are endowed with the power of healing and blessing (*baraka*), which they pass on to people. In exercising this function in practice as healers, they rely primarily on the tradition of curing diseases (*tibb an-nabi*) inherited from the Prophet Muhammad (PBUH).' Page 17.
46. Byron, *The Road to Oxiana*, 43.
47. Frembgen, *Journey to God*, 187.

48. Ibid.

49. Ibid., 185-6.

50. Ibid., 95.

51. National Database and Registration Authority.

52. Dalrymple, *White Mughals*, 221.

53. Esposito, *What Everyone Needs to Know about Islam*, second edition, 8-9.

54. Glasse, *The New Encyclopedia of Islam*, 121.

55. Campo, *Encyclopedia of Islam*, 201.

56. Ibid.

57. Ibid.

58. Frembgen, *Journey to God*, 71-73.

59. Ibid., 11.

60. Ibid., 120-121.

61. Ibid.

62. Ibid.

63. Ibid.

64. Read more about this in *From the Holy Mountain* by William Dalrymple.

65. Ibid., 123.

66. Ibid.

67. Ibid., 124.

68. Ibid., 123.

69. Dill, Walde, Graf, *Antike Mythen*, 402.

70. A government organization that looks after the major shrines of the country.

71. An eleventh-century Muslim saint from Baghdad, founder of the Qadriyyah sect, a dominant spiritual Sufi *silsila* in the Muslim world.

72. Chief Seattle's letter written to the President of the United

States Franklin Pierce in the year 1855.

73. Krishna, *Sacred Animals of India*, 194.

74. Ibid., 197.

75. Zahir ud din Babur, *Baburnama*, 381.

76. Iqbal Qaiser is the author of the book *Historical Sikh Shrines in Pakistan*, in which the history of this gurdwara is noted.

77. Qaiser, *Historical Sikh Shrines in Pakistan*, 288.

78. Rose, *A Glossary of the Tribes and Castes of the Punjab and North-West Frontier Province*, 617.

79. Frembgen, *Journey to God*, 76.

80. Ibid., 75.

81. Krishna, *Sacred Animals of India*, 93.

82. Kurzman, *Liberal Islam: A Source Book*, 121.

83. Campo, *Encyclopedia of Islam*, 131.

84. Frembgen, *Journey to God*, 114.

85. Naeem, *Naya Lahore*, 29-32.

86. Ibid.

87. For more discussion on this, read *Prejudice and Pride* by Krishna Kumar.

88. Qaiser, *Historical Sikh Shrines in Pakistan*, 370.

89. Krishna, *Sacred Animals of India*, 82.

90. Ali, *The Holy Quran: English Translation and Commentary*.

91. *Pakistan Archaeology Report*, 184.

92. http://hrisouthasian.org/index.php?option=com_content&view=article&id=35:peelu-the-f.

93. Chisti, *Tajul Auliya*, 49.

94. Frembgen, *Journey to God*, 75.

95. Ibid., 76.

≈

# Bibliography

Anonymous. *Cultus Arborum: A Descriptive Account of Phallic Tree Worship With Illustrative Legends, Superstitions and Usages.* Montana: Kissinger Publishing, 2004.

Abid, Sohail. *Peelu: The First Narrator of the Legend of Mirza-Sahiban.* Hri Institute for Southasian Research and Exchange. Available at http://www.hrisouthasian.org/resource-center/gandharva/6-lovelegend/35-peelu-the-first-narrator-of-the-legend-of-mirza-sahiban.html

Ali, Maulana M., trans. *The Holy Quran: English Translation and Commentary.* Available at http://ahmadiyya.org/english-quran-2010/trans-quran-web.pdf (accessed on 15 Feb. 2013).

Anonymous. *Cultus Arborum: A Descriptive Account of the Phallus Tree Worship with Illustrative Legends, Superstitions and Usages.* Available at http://books.google.com.pk/books?id=b4TwOn4lQp8C&pg=PA61&dq=acacia+tree+worship+in+hinduism&hl=en&sa=X&ei=ETq3ULnZCZHBswbowICICA&redir_esc=y#v=onepage&q=acacia%20tree%20worship%20in%20hinduism&f=false (accessed on 20 Jan. 2013).

Babur, Zahir ud Din Mohammad. *Babur Nama.* New Delhi: Penguin Classics, 2006.

Baxter, Craig, ed. *Pakistan on the Brink*. Available at https:// books.google.com.pk/books?id=CFNtVqYqAwEC&prints ec=frontcover&dq=Baxter,+Craig,+ed.+Pakistan+on+the+ Brink&hl=en&sa=X&ved=0CBwQ6AEwAGoVChMIosH jo-b6xgIVA88UCh2FIgYd#v=onepage&q=Baxter%2C%20 Craig%2C%20ed.%20Pakistan%20on%20the%20 Brink&f=false (accessed on 10 Feb. 2013).

Byron, Robert. *The Road to Oxiana*. London: Oxford University Press, 1937.

Campo, Juan E. *Encyclopedia of Islam*. New York: Infobase, 2009. Available at https://books.google.com.pk/books?id=OZbyz_ Hr-eIC&printsec=frontcover&dq=Campo,+Juan+E.+Encyclo pedia+of+Islam&hl=en&sa=X&ved=0CBoQ6AEwAGoVCh MIl-DRuOb6xgIVybwUCh2i6QbV#v=onepage&q=Campo% 2C%20Juan%20E.%20Encyclopedia%20of%20Islam&f=false (accessed on 7 Feb. 2013).

Chakravarti, Mahadev. *The Concept of Rudra Siva through the Ages*. New Delhi: Motilal Banarsidass, 1986. Available at https:// books.google.com.pk/books?id=yMFwMHH4HzMC&pg=PR8- IA1&dq=Chakravarti,+Mahadev.+The+Concept+of+ Rudra+Siva+through+the+Ages&hl=en&sa=X&ved =0CBoQ6AEwAGoVChMIzeXvoOb6xgIVRjcUCh1- PgCZ#v=onepage&q=Chakravarti%2C%20Mahadev.%20 The%20Concept%20of%20Rudra%20Siva%20through%20 the%20Ages&f=false (accessed on 23 Oct. 2012).

Dalrymple, William. *City of Djinns*. New Delhi: Penguin, 1993.

———. *White Mughals*. London: HarperCollins, 2002.

Dill, Ueli, Christine Walde and Fritz Graf. *Antike Mythen*. Berlin: Die Deutsche Nationalbibliothek Verzeichnet Diese Publikation, 2009. Available at https://books.google.com.

pk/books?id=ufmTU599Bf8C&printsec=frontcover&dq=Dill,
+Ueli,+Christine+Walde,+and+Fritz+Graf.+Antike+Mythe&hl
=en&sa=X&ved= oCBwQ6AEwAGoVChMIkIW96Ob6xgIVR
rMUCh 3J Gg-P#v = onepage & q = D ill% 2C% 20Ueli%2C%20
Christine%20Walde%2C%20and%20Fritz%20Graf.%20
Antike%20Mythe&f=false (accessed on 29 Nov. 2012).

Elgood, Heather. *Hinduism and Religious Art*. London: Cassell,
1999. Available at https://books.google.com.pk/books?id= cj2t
AwAAQBAJ&printsec=frontcover&dq=Elgood,+Heather. +Hin
duism+and+Religious+Art&hl=en&sa=X&ved=oCBoQ6AEwA
GoVChMI26Whhef6xgIViDwUChoeSgIk#v=onepage&q=Elgo
od%2C%20Heather.%20Hinduism%20and%20Religious%20
Art&f=false (accessed on 11 Jan. 2013).

Esposito, John L. *What Everyone Needs to Know about Islam*.
New York: Oxford University Press, 2002. Available at
https://books.google.com.pk/books? id=2wSVQ I3Ya2EC&
printsec = frontcover&dq=Esposito,+John+L.+What+Every
one+Needs+to+Know+about+Islam.&hl=en&sa=X&ved=o
CBsQ6AEwAGoVChMItKHDsef6xgIVTFYUChIlKAB4#v
=onepage&q=Esposito%2C%20John%20L.%20What%20
Everyone%20Needs%20to%20Know%20about%20
Islam.&f=false (accessed on 15 Jan. 2013).

Farooqi, Muhammad A. C. *Tajul Auliya*. Chistian: Markaz-e-
taleemat-e-Fareediya, 1991.

Fair, C. Christine. *The Madrassah Challenge*. Washington: United
States Institute of Peace, 2008. Available at https://books.
google.com.pk/books?id=yKatQwAACAAJ&dq=Fair,+C.+Chris
tine.+The+Madrassah+Challenge&hl=en&sa=X&ved=oCCEQ6
AEwAWoVChMIr6SOxuf6xgIVytcUCho_yQKo (accessed on
11 Feb. 2013).

Frembgen, Jürgen Wasim. *Journey to God.* Karachi: Oxford University Press, 2008.

Glasse, Cyril. *The New Encyclopedia of Islam.* London: Stacey International, 1989. Available at https://books.google.com. pk/books?id=focLrox-frUC&printsec=frontcover&dq=Glasse ,+Cyril.+The+New+Encyclopedia+of+Islam&hl=en&sa=X&v ed=0CBsQ6AEwAGoVChMIlcKL–f6xgIVRFkUCh1D7wiV# v=onepage&q=Glasse%2C%20Cyril.%20The%20New%20 Encyclopedia%20of%20Islam&f=false (accessed on 17 Feb. 2013).

Gupta, Om. *Encyclopedia of India, Pakistan and Bangladesh.* New Delhi: Isha, 2006. Available at https://books.google.com.pk/ books?id=VYInTMBQ9vQC&printsec=frontcover&dq=Gupt a,+Om.+Encyclopedia+of+India,+Pakistan+and+Bangladesh &hl=en&sa=X&ved=0CBoQ6AEwAGoVChMIiNbCk-j6xgIV irwUChoX6Av5#v=onepage&q=Gupta%2C%20Om.%20 Encyclopedia%20of%20India%2C%20Pakistan%20and%20 Bangladesh&f=false (accessed on 13 March 2013).

Jaffrelot, Christophe. *A History of Pakistan and Its Origin.* London: Anthem, 2002. Available at https://books.google. com.pk/books?id=Q9sI_Y2CKAcC&printsec=frontcover&d q=Jaffrelot,+Christophe.+A+History+of+Pakistan+and+Its+ Origin.&hl=en&sa=X&ved=0CBoQ6AEwAGoVChMIoZ-Kp-j6xgIVAcAUCh2W3Ase#v=onepage&q=Jaffrelot%2C%20 Christophe.%20A%20History%20of%20Pakistan%20 and%20Its%20Origin.&f=false (accessed on 15 March 2013).

James, Edwin Oliver. *The Tree of Life.* Leiden: Brill, 1966. Available at https://books.google.com.pk/books?id=GP75P3 CWmZ4C&pg=PR3&dq=James,+Edwin+Oliver.+The+Tree+o f+Life.+Leiden&hl=en&sa=X&ved=0CBoQ6AEwAGoVChM

Isr-1u-j6xgIVi9YUChiruwa_#v=onepage&q=James%2C%20
Edwin%20Oliver.%20The%20Tree%20of%20Life.%20
Leiden&f=false (accessed on 10 Feb. 2013).

Joshi, Dinkar. *Glimpses of Indian Culture.* New Delhi: Star
Publications, 2005. Available at https://books.google.com.
pk/books?id=-fw-0iBvmMAC&printsec=frontcover&dq=Josh
i,+Dinkar.+Glimpses+of+Indian+Culture&hl=en&sa=X&ved
=0CBoQ6AEwAGoVChMI66ijoOj6xgIVRl4UCho5Wwbk#v-
=onepage&q=Joshi%2C%20Dinkar.%20Glimpses%20of%20
Indian%20Culture&f=false (accessed on 27 Jan. 2013).

Kamran, Tahir. 'The Evolution of Deobandi Islam in the Punjab.'
*The Historian* (n.d.).

Kishore, B. R. *Lord Shiva.* New Delhi: Diamond Pocket, 2001.
Available at https://books.google.com.pk/books?id=Lkqf5Gru
pR8C&printsec=frontcover&dq=Kishore,+B.+R.+Lord+Shiva&
hl=en&sa=X&ved=0CBoQ6AEwAGoVChMIn8aigen6xgIVx1
wUCh1YvQzV#v=onepage&q=Kishore%2C%20B.%20R.%20
Lord%20Shiva&f=false (accessed on 19 Dec. 2012).

Krishna, Nanditha. *Sacred Animals of India.* New Delhi:
Penguin India, 2010. Available at https://books.google.com.
pk/ books?id=J3 NU35nngxEC&printsec=frontcover&dq=Kr
ishna,+Nanditha.+Sacred+Animals+of+India&hl=en&sa=X&
ved=0CBsQ6AEwAGoVChMI3Jqslen6xgIVBTkUCh3GYQ6
T#v=onepage&q=Krishna%2C%20Nanditha.%20Sacred%20
Animals%20of%20India&f=false (accessed on 15 Feb. 2013).

Kurzman, Charles. *Liberal Islam: A Source Book.* New York: Oxford
University Press, 1998. Available at https://books.google.com.
pk/books?id= 4n8HSe9SfXMC&printsec=frontcover&dq=Kurz
man,+Charles.+Liberal+Islam:+A+Source+Book&hl=en&sa=X
&ved=0CBoQ6AEwAGoVChMIhp61wen6xgIVxboUChoxHg

ps#v=onepage&q=Kurzman%2C%20Charles.%20Liberal%20
Islam%3A%20A%20Source%20Book&f=false (accessed on 2
March 2013).

Naeem, Muhammad. *Naya Lahore*. Lahore: Shalimar Publication,
2004.

Pruthi, Rajkumar. *Indus Civilization*. New Delhi: Discovery
Publishing House, 2004. Available at https://books.google.
com.pk/books?id=XgFu-9UFoTYC&pg=PA252&dq=indus+
civilization+by+raj+kumar+pruthi&hl=en&sa=X&ved=0CB
oQ6AEwAGoVChMIj-fo6Or6xgIViroUCh2opgRj#v=onep
age&q=indus%20civilization%20by%20raj%20kumar%20
pruthi&f=false (accessed on 12 Feb. 2013).

Qaiser, Iqbal. *Historical Sikh Shrines in Pakistan*. Lahore: Punjabi
History Board, 1998.

Rana, Junaid Akram. *Terrifying Muslims*. Durham: Duke
University Press, 2011. Available at https://books.google.
com.pk/books?id=jfFGJmCU5I4C&pg=PA230&dq=Rana,+Ju
naid+Akram.+Terrifying+Muslims&hl=en&sa=X&ved=0CBo
Q6AEwAGoVChMI39bngOv6xgIVy28UChoDUgRF#v=onep
age&q=Rana%2C%20Junaid%20Akram.%20Terrifying%20
Muslims&f=false (accessed on 17 Feb. 2013).

Rasool, Niaz, ed. *Pakistan Archaeology*. Vol. 29. Karachi:
Department of Archaeology, 1996.

Rose, Horace Aurthur. *A Glossary of the Tribes and Castes of the
Punjab and North-West Frontier Province*. New Delhi: Asian
Educational Services, 1990. Available at https://archive.org/
details/glossaryoftribes03rose (accessed on 4 March 2013).

Seattle, Chief. 'Chief Seattle: 1855.' Context Institute. Available
at http://www.context.org/iclib/ic03/seattle/ (accessed on 11
Nov. 2012).

Shaw, Miranda. *Buddhist Goddesses of India*. New Jersey: Princenton UP, 2006. Available at https://books.google.com. pk/books?id=MvDKOK1h3zMC&printsec=frontcover&dq=Shaw,+Miranda.+Buddhist+Goddesses+of+India&hl=en&sa=X&ved=0CB0Q6AEwAGoVChMI8sq-6uv6xgIVAWoUCh3skAbv#-v=onepage&q=Shaw%2C%20Miranda.%20Buddhist%20Goddesses%20of%20India&f=false (accessed on 21 Dec. 2012).

Singh, Kahan. *Encyclopedia of Sikh Literature*. Patiala: Bhasha Wibhaga, Pañjaba, 1960.

Sleeman, William Henry. *Rambles and Recollections of an Indian Official*. London: Hatchard, 1844. Available at https://books. google.com.pk/books?id=5dMMAAAAIAAJ&printsec=frontcover&dq=Sleeman,+William+Henry.+Rambles+and+Recollections+of+an+Indian+Officia&hl=en&sa=X&ved=0CB0Q6AEwAGoVChMIq6b-_uv6xgIVicMUChoMjgFF#v=onepage&q=Sleeman%2C%20William%20Henry.%20Rambles%20and%20Recollections%20of%20an%20Indian%20Officia&f=false (accessed on 21 Jan. 2013).

Thursby, Gene R. *Hindu-Muslim Relations in British India: A Study of Controversy, Conflict and Communal Movements in Northern India, 1923-1928*. Leiden: Brill, 1975. Available at https://books.google.com.pk/books?id=abcfAAAAIAAJ&printsec=frontcover&dq=Thursby,+Gene+R.+Hindu-Muslim+Relations+in+British+India&hl=en&sa=X&ved=0CB0Q6AEwAGoVChMIzdO6mOz6xgIVQlcUCh2ajwzt#v=onepage&q=Thursby%2C%20Gene%20R.%20Hindu-Muslim%20Relations%20in%20British%20India&f=false (accessed on 11 Feb. 2013).

≈